MOMENT OF INSIGHT

MOMENT OF INSIGHT

Vignettes from a Psychoanalytic Practice

SUMNER L. SHAPIRO, M.D.

INTERNATIONAL UNIVERSITIES PRESS, INC.
New York

To my wife, my children,
and all my other teachers

Library of Congress Cataloging in Publication Data

Shapiro, Sumner L
    Moment of insight.

    1. Psychoanalysis—Cases, clinical reports, statistics. I. Title. [DNLM: 1. Psychiatry. 2. Psychoanalytic therapy. WM460 S529m]
RC504.S5   616.8'917'0926   76-42277
ISBN 0-8236-3442-6

CONTENTS

Preface   ix

Introduction   xi

1 *My Death Had Been the Healthiest One
    in Her Life*   1

2 *Monkey See, Monkey Do*   13

3 *The Thief*   19

4 *The Philadelphia Lawyer*   35

On Accidents   43

5 *The Boston Strangler*   45

6 *The Boomerang*   63

7 *Three Strikes, You're Out*   67

8 *Sonya and the Monster*   75

9 *The Anatomy of a Moron*   101

Preface

Years ago, so many there's an interface of fantasy and fact, I either read or dreamed a story. In it an inventor built an apparatus that could gather, then rebroadcast long lost words. Its construction was ingenious: by adjusting dials and needles one could resurrect King Arthur or the Gettysburg address, or by tuning different wave lengths reproduce the plays of Shakespeare at the Globe.

What a lovely pipedream! And how wanton! For the dreadful fact is that sounds and speech are written on the wind—they die with the fading echoes and are gone. Words, to be preserved, need recording somehow, somewhere—that awareness justifies this book.

Introduction

Why this book? What motivated me to write it? Well, there were many reasons, but the stimulus I really needed came in 1969.

In that year the climate in which I'd been working was becoming smoggy, and my forty years of training, my prestige, even my socially redeeming value, all at a blow, were being threatened and impugned. Where once to hold the vaunted title "psychoanalyst" was passport to respect and adulation (second only to "Supreme Court justice"), now to do so had but little worth in a public sentiment grown doubtful and hostile. My profession, if not openly derided, often was disguisedly but viciously lampooned.

Like other psychiatrists I had heard the rumor that analysis was in trouble. The post World War II boom, which had seen the enfranchising of many new psychoanalytic institutes throughout the country and the world and which had recruited so many enthusiastic adherents, not only had leveled off, but was said to be showing signs of gradual attrition.

Former Freudian believers were busy looking for faster, less expensive therapies, and a revitalized civilization, geared to the exciting scientific spinoff of the war, understandably felt little patience for lying every day on a couch to talk of dreams. Throughout the nation shorter, cheaper, more flamboyant new treatments were springing up. All of them brashly implied that they could do it better and for less. For the most part they repudiated any historic linkage with, or obligation to, the basic psychoanalytic themes on which they played their variations. In so doing, they shamelessly kicked the shins of their less obtrusive classic ancestor.

Proponents of a peculiar faddist school of primal therapy were intimating that they, not Freud, had discovered what he, eighty years before, called "catharsis." Behaviorists, while touting their "conditioning," apparently ignored the analytic "working through" and "synthesis" so kindred to it. Sensitivity trainees, in heralding themselves unique, both talked and wrote as if the traditional corpus had never dealt with confrontations, our building blocks for insights and the final cure.

Here in Los Angeles, I repeatedly overheard enthusiastic chatter about "marathons," "encounter groups," and "weekend pressure cookers." Within them, allegedly, defenses could be made to melt away and personality, once liquefied, allowed to find and flow into new healthy channels. Instant character, like instant coffee or cement, was being marketed as a commodity available to breathless businessmen and harried housewives through the bypass of group meetings, moral suasion, physical exhaustion, and a spate of magic "buzz" words.

None of which is meant, one instant, to deny that some of the converts to the newer schools were quite devoted and serious social scientists—even if surrounded by blatant charlatans against whose raucous preachings the soft-spoken analyst had small chance of being heard. To add to my distress, even from within their ranks the intelligentsia had started poking fun. The net result, of course—as ever when a civil war takes place—the hapless victims were the innocent bystanders, the beleaguered patients who couldn't judge to which side they ought to turn. Small wonder that legitimate psychotherapies were also muddied by the flood and that resistance, at best a naturally formidable barrier among the laity, became intensified beyond all bounds.

The entire "movement" of that time was perhaps epitomized in an exhaustive article in the widely circulated *Playboy Magazine*.[1] Read in its entirety by a scholar, it would have proved a generally favorable piece, supporting our travail, but, skimmed while lying on the beach, a highball in one hand, it could easily be misconstrued as yet another deadly knock on the reeling giant's head.

I wrote to the editors of that magazine detailing just such sentiments and lamenting that my field was being further hurt, misunderstood. I was even more deeply troubled when I reflected on how few people really knew the facts, or had clear access to them, or knew the hardships and devotion necessary for a man to qualify for the certificates I held—so much the analytic leitmotif had always been low profile, blending in the woodwork. And it upset me to realize that only the merest handful knew the precision, the delicacy, the patience, the dang-

[1] Hunt, M. M., Crisis in Psychoanalysis. *Playboy Magazine,* 16, Oct. 1969, pp. 107, 108, 116, 174-76, 178, 180.

ers, and the artistry involved. How come? Well, perhaps the fault was ours.

The typical psychoanalyst (if indeed there be such) is a man so prone to cherish his unflappable image, and to respect the utter confidentiality to which he's sworn, that he maintains his silence even to his disadvantage. He does so in the face of all he meets; rather than retort, he analyzes. He hesitates to dignify most accusations with a reply; there is no need. The way of wisdom calls for poise, decorum—silence. One doesn't use artillery to squash a gnat!

Yet mightn't preservation of that image easily be construed as passivity, compliance? Mind, I understand the history and guiding principles behind both the reticence and anonymity. They are tools meant to foster a patient's projection and to allow him to imagine us as what he most needs us to be, without the contradiction of widely publicized facts. For such reasons I never volunteer if I'm a Democrat, Protestant, Easterner, baseball fan, or chess fiend; rather, I encourage each to imagine what he will to suit his needs.

However, there comes a point beyond which taciturnity transmutes to pathologic. When your beloved is attacked you have the right, if not the obligation, to cry out. It seemed appropriate to broadcast the fact that it is rare to be a full-fledged psychoanalyst before the fifth decade of one's life. How come? College, graduate school, medical school, internship, residency training, personal analysis, institute matriculation, seminars, supervised casework, colloquia—they all add up to almost half a century in pursuit of one's degrees. So, wasn't it justifiable to lament and feel a bit indignant if the laity, uncomprehending, began to jade and jape about my work?

I felt it was, intensely, and I sought a way, a way within the bounds of tactfulness and the promised confidentiality to clarify some misconceptions and speak out. I wondered, could there be some manner in which I might take the public in behind my couch and desk to have a first-hand glance at what I do and why? To let it eavesdrop ethically and overhear the sentient, the tragic, the dramatic (and the humdrum) to which I'm privy? And to do so in a way to plead my case?

Well, by a happy coincidence, even as I mulled over these matters, I was offered the editorship of a tiny psychoanalytic magazine. Despite its skinny frame and anemic circulation, it inadvertently furnished me the answers and impetus I sought. In it I published stories of the patients I had treated. They found instant favor among my fellow therapists and several other members of educated groups. Some notoriety was gained.

Then it occurred to me that these very stories might be a vehicle through which I could reach an audience of much wider radius still. By them, better than any theoretical diatribe, I could document, explain, rebut.

These I offer now to serve as spokesman for myself and my gentlemanly colleagues of the analytic schools— without harangue or vitriol, as befits the image, yet, I hope, with the impact of a *Fifty Minute Hour*, a *Sybil*, or the *Three Faces of Eve*. Reproduced within this volume are experiences from my practice. Each, of course, is much disguised to conceal identities; each enjoys a little dramatic license, yet each is essentially true. And should I add the hope that each may bring to the reader some small extra appreciation of the uniqueness and the merits of what I consider the most fulfilling work in the world?

1

My Death Had Been the Healthiest One in Her Life

I was surprised to hear Nancy's voice. It was deeper and more sophisticated. Why not? After all, she had been a very young lady when I had treated her, and that was some time ago.

It was about her Uncle Lester's death.

From her analysis I knew of his brilliant career and could well picture how the family might react to his loss. Little surprise that Grandma, who had already buried her husband and first-born in "the Old Country" was especially hard hit. Nancy feared that Grandma wouldn't survive this shock and asked if there was anything I could

First published in *Psychiatric Quarterly*, 46(1):22-28. Reprinted by permission.

recommend. But beyond a few embarrassingly trite platitudes and my sincere commiseration, there seemed little to offer.

A week later Nancy's mother phoned. "Forgive my annoying you, Doctor. Nan's back at school, so I made bold to call. It's Mother. She's having a very hard time over my brother's death. I know that it isn't your usual practice, but she's heard so much of you from Nan, we thought that under the circumstances you could just talk a little with her. She often said that she wanted to meet you."

To refuse such a consultation on the basis of "psychoanalytic purity" would have been utterly pointless, and cruel, yet it was equally so to encourage it, as Grandma's grief appeared wholly justified. In agreeing to see her I had gross misgivings as to what could be done for an octogenarian with such a legitimate claim to depression, and when the appointed hour rolled around, annoyed with myself for compliance, I tried to control a gloomy futility. That was one feeling Grandma would least need.

Three o'clock. One minute past. Then two, then five. The red sweep of the second hand kept moving. Ten after. No one yet.

Certain that the family understood the usual punctuality problem, I wondered (and hoped). Could something have happened to change the plan? An alternative?

Not so. There were sounds of approaching feet, and a slow but steady opening of the door, and then—there she was, Grandma.

It is always fascinating, even fulfilling, when a true flesh-and-blood personification appears, someone whose image you have constructed through another's perceptions. Nancy had described her grandmother frequently, and not inaccurately. And now there she stood like a mythologic character magically inspired with life, a wax museum figure made to move, breathe, and speak.

"So. You are the doctor?"

"I am, and how do you do," I managed, as it flashed through my mind that just as she for me, so I too for her was metamorphosing from myth and wax to blood, flesh, and bone.

"Shake hands. I'm pleased to make your acquaintance," she said.

I gazed upon Grandma. Mrs. "Five-by-five"—or better perhaps, Mrs. "Five-by-five-by-five." A perfect cube of a woman, compressed into a solid, much-aged, somewhat distorted, yet still unmistakable Nancy.

Seeing and liking her were instantaneous, and I bade her to sit.

"Sit I will, Doctor, but stay, I don't know. You see, it wasn't my idea, this visit. What's the use? Can you bring back my son?"

Behind the thick cataract lenses, lubricating the fleshy wrinkles of her face, there sprung up two ample streams of tears. And as she sat, she sobbed and shook, a portrayal of grief.

Isn't it curious how we hunger for comic relief when an atmosphere is so pervaded with sorrow? No doubt some cosmic good sense accounts for it, but enough that a fantastic contrast was presented in the tragic charade of the bereaved mother and the ludicrous spectacle of the way she calculated, steered, guided, then dropped herself into the deep Danish-Modern seat.

Grandma's stubby, short legs hardly reached the floor; as to the rest of her, she filled the space like a liquid. And there she sat, patently mourning, covertly pleading, even defying.

"So, can you bring him back? No, it wasn't my idea to come here, dear Doctor. I know your time is valuable, and I know you should spend it on younger people . . . with more hope. For me there is nothing."

And nothing was my reply.

"It isn't the first time. Oh no, believe me! You're a young man, and I don't know, have you tasted tragedy? God help you if so. Don't mind if I talk personal. I take the privilege of old people—but God should help you if you know from experience what it is. My husband, now it's thirty years, and still I'm not over that, also in his prime, and so good. And then my son. But still it's not enough! So now my angel. That's more than an old woman can bear . . . Are you married, dear Doctor? Do you have children? I know you don't answer; that's what I see on T.V. No answers. Yeh, can you bring him back? No, aaagh!"

Grandma turned to the window and sponged away at a fresh flow of tears. Even had I had something to offer, she didn't give me the chance: "So, what can you do for me? Do you know what? All that can be done for me now is to die. And I'll tell you a secret: that I pray every night I shouldn't wake in the morning. That's what. I pray to die . . . my golden son!

"Let me tell you—no, probably Nancy already did—his talents: so patient, so thoughtful. I hate to say it, but that one was the best of all my children. Oh, not to say something against my daughter, only since her divorce and all. You know, I trust you, so I'll say. I never could 'modernize' like the divorces—and she is a fine woman, you understand. But my angel—that was a one!

"He had a kind word for everybody. They wanted him to run for mayor, and believe me, for a Jewish boy that wouldn't be easy in Tower City. Everyone loved him. And patience! Nothing was too much. You could wake that one at three in the morning and ask a favor, and he smiles and asks, 'Are you sure that's all?' Not to say something against his wife. But, that's another story . . .

"Oi, oi, oi."

It seemed impertinent to interrupt. Grandma was telling the tale she had undoubtedly told herself a thousand times silently since his death.

"'Patience' was his middle name. I don't want to knock the others, mind you, but even from Tower City, which ain't around the corner, every Friday noon he drove himself thirty miles to get me. Always Friday. And always the wife whom I am very fond, and his beautiful children, for the ride. But it's me he took to Temple. So busy he was, he was never too busy for that."

Grandma stopped. She rocked back and forth in a manner perhaps identical with her praying at those services. She wept. "So, why do I take your time, Doctor? What can you do for me? Hum? Yeh, you are a good listener; Nancy told me. Now I'm quiet. You say."

"What is there to say?" I ventured, aware of the futility of the question.

"Yeah, what? Such a boy! With thieves and gangsters and crooks running around and my angel not. Does it make sense? Does it? Every night I look at his picture, my beautiful son, and kiss it, and cry myself to sleep. I am dry; no more tears; just noises. And can you believe it? I pray to God to take me. So—tell me. Something.

"Nancy said you were quiet. She really respected you. I see why . . . How old are you, Doctor? Just his age,

I bet; ha, even a little you resemble. Oi, how foolish an old fool can be."

She daubed at her tears, then started up again.

"Look, something I want to tell you; you'll see how foolish a Grandma you have. I am ashamed to say it even, but who loses so much already—what can I lose more?"

She looked away, then slowly turned back to me.

The old woman hesitated, drew a deep breath, and reassured herself that what she was about to reveal was safe. "The wife, my daughter-in-law, how did it happen? I am ashamed to say. And not that I didn't try to love her, for his sake. She is a hard type, and always I thought not the one he could be happiest with. Not that I am narrow-minded about her religion, because I read books in my day and am a modern type. Even he used to say so, but she was not for him. It didn't matter she converted. Who wouldn't for such a jewel?

"Listen. She couldn't have children. I mean not her own. They adopted. Yeh, that's for me a disappointment too, but you bear in life. Even him I never told, or anyone. But that hurt. Her tubes, I don't know what. And sometimes they were, well, like children will be, cranky, fussy. *She* didn't have the patience to manage them.

"Oh, my son, like I told you, an angel, he would reason; she would hit. I saw it with my own eyes!

"So now you'll see what a big fool I am. Friday he called. 'Ma, I'll get you at one o'clock and we'll go to Temple. Okay?' 'No,' I said. 'What's the matter, Ma?' he asks me. And I told him a lie.

"The truth? I tell you; you will see what a fool can do.

"Him I didn't tell; who wants him to worry? But over a silly nothing that keeps me up all Thursday night. Because the old schnorrer doesn't invite me to play cards at his table. And me, like I'm sixteen, I'm hurt, and I don't shut my eyes a wink that night, and God help me, I'm too irritable to put up with the wife, the kids, the noises, the fights, so I tell him, 'Next week, Darling.' And next week he is dead and buried."

Grandma wept afresh; she moaned. In the tight compartment of her seat she found space to quiver. I watched, moved and goose-pimply. Something had troubled me in what I'd heard, something which then began to give way to encouragement. It was that last little confession about her having put off her son. That might prove a hopeful twist to an otherwise grim story.

The office clock showed that we were obliged to stop, but it was now clear that Grandma was feeling guilty. Her pride, her self-indulgent pride, had had a hand in preventing a last living encounter with her son. Of course it was impossible to bring him back, but with luck I just might be able to help her with this awful recrimination. Accordingly, waiving whatever protocol applied, I really urged her to return.

*   *   *

So there were second and third visits. Then there were more. Grandma was grieving, appropriately, aloud, regularly, and with welcome acceptance rather than the tolerant impatience others afforded her. An extra dividend of the therapy was the expiation over having rejected her son during their last telephone encounter.

Together we went over the story. Usually she apologized for having told it to me before. Invariably I reassured her that it was good to repeat herself and showed her how frequently each repetition offered some fresh little consideration, an added confession, an embellishment, with more insight and relief.

Each time she seemed a trifle better for the retelling. "Better," that is, only in a sense, inasmuch as her improvement was not altogether a welcome commodity. In fact it proved an interesting aside and commentary on human nature. In the nursing home where she was resident, she had been so very withdrawn during the depths of depression that whatever was served at mealtime sufficed. She didn't complain about the broken television set and accepted the malfunctioning of the air conditioner with nonchalance. However, as her mood lifted, the personnel found her "troublesome and demanding." The psychological triumph proved a sociologic defeat!

And then it happened.

Everything seemed as usual, except that Grandma arrived with a bundle under her arm. It gave me the cue to comment, "You have a package, I see," as she eased herself into her chair.

"Yeah, I'll catch my breath, then show you."

"What is it?"

"What it is you'll see, dear Doctor."

"Okay. When you're ready."

"Ready. Here—look, an angel! Ain't he beautiful?" With which, in a single motion, she unwrapped and handed me a gold-framed portrait of the hero of our story. "That's him."

She watched me study it, then her, then it again. I remarked aloud on the resemblance, and she reminded me that this was the photograph she spoke to and kissed "good night" each night.

"But I don't do that anymore, Doctor."

"No?"

"No! No more."

"You have stopped, hm?"

"Yeh, but something ..."

"Something? What something?"

"Something like only an old fool could do, and only a bigger fool would say."

"What are you getting at?" I asked.

"I am saying what is for a silly old woman to say, and say it I will: that now I don't kiss him anymore at night."

"And is that silly?" I questioned.

"Not that—that even I think is healthy. Silly is that now, dear Doctor, at night when I go to sleep I see another face. A sweet face, and I talk to it."

"Another sweet face?"

"Yours!"

"Mine?"

"Yours. I talk to you for hours. I tell you of my mother's boarding house when we arrived in this country, about the winters in Galicia, about the Russian pogroms and the Cossack horsemen. How we moved so many times to keep one step ahead of tragedy, and how it was already there waiting when we arrived. Who knows what else? I talk; and I do not blush to say that I love you. Like a son. So, am I not a big fool? Don't answer; hear first what, because I don't come back here after today. Soon my daughter picks me up, and I tell you *auf wiedersehen;* that's German 'good-bye.' "

Grandma smiled. "Now," she said, "Say!"

I too smiled, "What shall I say?"

"Nu, like you always tell me—'Say what you're thinking.' "

I laughed aloud, then replied, "Okay. I'll tell you what I'm thinking—and I want you to listen very carefully. If you don't understand, stop me and I'll explain it another way, all right?"

"Why not?"

"Okay. Perhaps it is a good idea to stop now, or soon, perhaps not. I'm uncertain. But one thing I am sure is necessary, is for you to understand why you have arranged to call it quits so suddenly. Do you know?"

"Why to stop? You're the doctor. You tell me."

"I'll try, but first I want your promise that you'll hear me out, even if we have to get you back another time."

"So tell me," said the old woman.

"Well, it isn't really so complicated. I think that you've come to be very much attached to me, and that you gradually have turned onto me all the affection that you used to lavish on your son. At night you have allowed me to take his place at your bedside, when you have those long talks with me."

"So far I understand. And agree," she added.

"Yes, but that's not all. You know, at least three times in your life you have grown to love someone, and without a warning, he has been taken away from you— am I right?"

"So far, clear."

"Right. And do you know what more I think?"

"Yeh?"

"I think that you are afraid that if you don't pull out quickly while you're ahead, that just the same as happened to you with the others, will happen to you with me. You're afraid that you'll maybe get too attached to me, and I'll die just as your husband and two sons. Then you'll be hurt again—the old pattern. Do you see?"

"God love you, Doctor! You read my mind."

"No, not really. Anyway what matters is that you understand it and realize that you don't have to be as superstitious as all that, or as guilty. Your thoughts and fears won't kill me at all. It's for that reason I want you to continue for just a little more, so I can convince you of what I've just said."

"Our time is up so soon?"

"Today, yes, but come next week and we'll go over it again."

Grandma agreed, and, with what I construed as a mawkish and seductive grin and a little lilt in her voice, said, "Good-bye."

In the session that followed I worked over the same idea with her in many ways and with several clinical and practical examples. I tried to show her how it was natural for her to need to repeat actively what passively she had been made victim of on those previous occasions. I taught her how man always tries to do just that to gain mastery over an overwhelming shock.

And she grasped the entire concept, with insight as to how it applied to her in this instance as well as in others, seeing how it was necessary to make me her son as a device of mourning—all of which was accompanied by a really gratifying clinical improvement. Indeed, her depression lifted so much, that the nursing home literally wanted no more of her and asked her family to take her out—which done, the meetings ended and the relationship between us.

Or did it?

I shall probably never wholly know, for when we stood together in the doorway for the last time, something in her glance made me just a bit uneasy, even though I didn't feel it out of place that so old and sentimental a patient take "the privilege of age" and kiss my cheek. And for all the effort, the theory, the exceptions, the variations, the unfinished, I did feel that when the door shut behind her, my old friend went back to her world a little better than when we met, and that my death had been the healthiest one in her life.

2
Monkey See,
Monkey Do

His problem: he left the priesthood to get married to a nun who did the same. A really sweet young man, if easily embarrassed. A funny blend of depth with immaturity. Small surprise he should need guidance for his guilt and feeling of awkwardness in his new role. Just back from his honeymoon, bearded, long-locked, looking paradoxically more like Jesus now than he ever did before, he squirmed a little on the couch, anticipating what would come out.

"Yeah. Well, here I am again. And I suppose I've gotta tell you all my thoughts—including how things went. Do you remember how nervous I was? I'm sure you do. And how hung up?

"I know the rules. Okay, here goes: I was nauseous about sex. The missionary' part—well, I could live with that, but all the 'foreplay' stuff. I wanted, like you said,

13

to be just natural, do what we pleased, but I was uptight as a cat. I wanted, and I didn't, both at once.

"We drove two thousand miles, at least. That much was great. Mountains, Carlsbad Caverns—but every time I tuned in to my thoughts it all came back. The priesthood and the Church, and how I made my mind up and I was married now . . . and had my rights. And I was gonna' *say* that to *my wife*.

"We were driving east through Utah on this really empty road when I said, 'Sweetheart, there's something that we've gotta discuss.' Know what? Right there, I froze, solid. The words were ice cubes in my throat.

"Well, she looked at me, those sad big eyes and that pale face—I could've bet she knew exactly what I meant to say. Instead, she asked if I wanted her to light me a cigarette.

"Some smoker! She tried to, but a little patch of paper stuck to her lip when she flipped it to me; it bled. So she put the cigarette in the ash tray in the dash—unlit.

"Gallant me! I kissed my fingertip and put it on her 'boo-boo' and told her to forget the smoke—instead to slide across the seat and cuddle up. And she was sleepy so she put her head down in my lap and she was gone.

"And while she dozed that way my eyes kept sneeking peeks at her—the contour of her body. I was fascinated with the way her bosom swelled and rose each time she breathed and how her thighs were pressed together and the place they disappeared up in her skirt. Then I stroked her hair. And I kept muttering, 'my wife.'

"But let me clue you in to how my mind worked. She lay there like I used to dream she would. And it occurred to me, alone, so little traffic on the road, I could . . . what a chance! Why I could test if my odometer was accurate. I meant to ever since I'd bought the car—just keep her set on sixty and see if she would cover one full mile in sixty seconds flat. Was I a chicken? You bet your life!

"I got to thinking back to sex and foreplay. Well, that night we would, for sure! I lit myself a cigarette and smoked it and, almost like to prove my point, I snubbed it out by breaking it in half. Right in the middle, you know? It made two pieces. One of them came up against the other that my wife had laid in the tray. And when I saw the two of them, my cigarette was like kneeling at her feet. A supplicant—before his stately queen. Hers a little blood-stained but otherwise 'unused'; the damp tip of mine against the midsection of hers—you see?

And that reminded me about her in the shower earlier that morning. What I should have done is knocked and gone right in. Do you know what the priesthood's like? 'Give me a child the first five years.'

"Later when we stopped to eat I had another smoke and so did she. And this time I was careful how I put my cigarette. I laid it there full length alongside hers, and gently, while she watched me, sort of curious what I was up to, I squeezed the filter tips together and blew a kiss to her. Know what? She shuddered like you see girls do.

"Back in the driver's seat I had it all worked out. I would tell her how in therapy I'd learned the 'facts of life'—how you explained 'mutual consent' to me and how it's okay to do what you both want—whatever feels good. Only when I started my speech the words were syrup, thick and slow.

"Sweetheart, *we have got to talk!* You know I see an analyst. And then I blurted out the story you told me— about the man whose parents raised him so properly that later it would turn him on just saying 'bathroom words' and how he got his wife to work him up by shouting 'doggie doo' and 'kitty doo' and 'baby doo.'

"We both laughed and laughed. And just right then we passed a great big sign about a desert museum only fifty yards ahead.

"I didn't really chicken out. I mean the both of us were looking for adventures, and we both love animals, and I could always pick it up where I left off, right after we came out.

"Know what? I never had to anyhow. Know why? Well, in this cage they had a monkey. Really cute and smart, almost human—tiny thing. He saw my wife's sunglasses and he wanted them. He cooed and begged. He jumped up and down and stuck his scrawny little arm right out through the wire mesh to reach them. I said, 'Honey go ahead. You put them in his hand. See what he does. It's safe—there's no way he can pull them through.'

"*She* did. Know what *he* did? He dropped them to the ground and slid them underneath the bar inside the cage.

"Boy, that was all! He let loose a laugh and swung up on his shelf and squatted on his tailbone and put them on and off; he really got worked up. I know because his 'thing' came out, stood up, all red and swollen.

"And you know what he did then? He bent up double and he started rubbing it then licking it, his tongue right on his 'thing.'

"Yeah! Well, I looked down at my wife and she looked back. The cigarettes, the shower, the story I'd just told her, all of them and now this monkey making a monkey out of me. So I put my hand where hers was and I started to speak but, well, she like beat me to it. And with a tiny shaky voice I heard her asking, 'Sweetheart, does my *Monkey see?'*

"What else could I reply but, *'Monkey do!'"*

3
The Thief

A telephone was ringing. The nearest extension far up the hill was behind a locked door. It rang a third, fourth, and fifth time, then stopped abruptly on a lingering echo.

"Dammit! Dammit!" Bruno cried, throwing his pitchfork to the ground. Anna had told him, "Bruno, the yuccas by the pool. You take them out. I'll call later to see." And Bruno, with few excuses since retirement, was complying, resentfully.

Americanization had made Anna leader—her wishes were his commands. So, when the phone rang anew, poised beside it, Bruno sprang for the defenseless instrument. He was completely unbalanced by the curt message:

"Bruno, it's me, Anna. You come. I've been arrested."

That morning his wife had gone to town to visit Karen, her oldest girlfriend. That was the one who first couldn't find a husband, then for ten years tried to get a child, until—in fact that was it—Bruno recalled that Anna had gone to console her about the miscarriage. But "arrested"? That didn't make sense.

If he drove through the pass, Brendon would take half an hour. Pulling off his sweaty shorts, Bruno threw them into a corner of the bedroom. Reconsidering, with exaggerated delicacy, he retrieved and properly dropped them into the hamper in mock concession to Anna's meticulousness—a trait she had retained from her work as a domestic.

Grumbling, he rejected shaving but dressed speedily, and within minutes heard the automatic fuel injectors of his huge Mercedes hum reassuringly as a whisp of blue smoke puffed from its rear.

* * *

At the station the duty officer, Sergeant Power, presented a rugged, handsome, squared-away figure. Allowed only a "small moustache neatly trimmed" in the Marines, he was enjoying the more liberal Brendon Police Force policy, which tolerated its flushing out into the thick pile against which he now pressed a long, sharp yellow pencil. Using it as a baton, he conducted his booming bass voice in vigorous rendition.

"I'm personally sorry, Madam, but you're to be formally charged. There's nothing I can do. Shoplifting is a felony punishable by law. You've had the phone call allowed under it; your husband may contact your lawyer when he arrives. In the meantime, make yourself comfortable."

Outwardly calm, yet internally awry, Anna settled into a vigil, whimsically contrasting Bruno's passive aggression with the sergeant's active self-assertion. Rectitude personified, she sat geometrically, shoes parallel, legs perpendicular, knees two right angles, her torso squared on top, immobile, purse in lap. Inside her tranquil mannequin frenzied fantasies spun her out beyond the confines to Bruno, then Karen, and the events of the morning.

*   *   *

She was aware that what she was about to do was crazy, but she had absolutely no control. What drove her? Why were her protests so feeble, and how did she know that despite them the act was a *fait-accompli*? A mysterious premonition foretold that she would pull the big brass knob of the huge rococo door, walk straight in and unswervingly to Ladies' Wear, take the white two-piece cotton blouse and skirt to the dressing room, stuff them in her purse, and run. Run as if she were a robot programmed to a script she knew by heart.

Why in her trance had she bothered to notice the elderly man sitting, waiting, his white goatee resting on his fist leaning on his cane? He reminded her distressingly of a vague someone from the distant past.

Why was she so struck that the room was musty despite air-conditioning? Or that in the background musical tones kept summoning a salesgirl?

Why her alarm that the youngster who waited upon

her so oddly resembled Karen—the hairy mole at the angle of the lip, the tortoise-shell glasses, the stockings that made doughnuts just below her knee?

"Yes, the two-piece; may I try it on? No, not too small. I don't think . . . just right. Please, where is the dressing room? Thank you." Close the door. Ach, I'm perspiring. This is crazy. Purse open—in, in, so! Ha, done! My goodness look at the bulge. So, done. Can I breathe?

Then out of the dressing room saying, "No, I don't want it. Yes, it's in there on a hanger, thank you. Maybe I'll look more over there," while silently asking, "Was she looking at my bag? No matter. Walk fast—oh, is someone behind? Out of the door."

"What! You're the detective? Come with you back in? You like to examine my purse? I don't make any trouble. I'll come."

* * *

Anna's clean record, her lawyer's rhetoric, and the fact that she had cash, checks, and credit cards on her person, all convinced the authorities that more than punishment she needed psychiatric consultation. Such were the circumstances of our meeting. Yet, truth be told, at that first encounter, more than a thief, and certainly more than a patient, she seemed a soldier awaiting court-martial.

She stood there—a youthful, proud, pert, well-trained, European mercenary, arms akimbo, feet eighteen inches apart, left hip thrust forward, poised to tilt with anything or anyone. Off-setting the military air, a little felt skull cap perched jauntily atop her Dutch-cut blond bangs. Both the bangs and cap, but especially the latter, with its saw-toothed edge, were clearly homemade.

"I'm to be your doctor," I offered, to which, moving like a gymnast, she leaned to shake my hand, and defiantly telegraphed her remark.

"So, I'm to be examined. Well, let's get on with it."

I told Anna that my aim was to uncover emotional factors related to the shoplifting, that any help she could give me would facilitate the process, and that she should speak with complete freedom since I promised full confidentiality. Later, based upon what we learned I would make some recommendations after discussing them with her.

"And are you recording my words now?" she snapped.

"Certainly not. Nor do I intend to. That would never win your trust or anyone else's. Believe me, I'm not a spy, policeman, judge, or executioner, just a physician, a psychiatrist."

These words eased her some, but in what followed I could easily recognize how, in giddying alternation, I was being identified with just that parade of professionals—least of all the last. Anna said that she had done a "stupid, stupid thing," that she felt contrition and had never anticipated the enormous inconvenience. She assured me she was not crazy and would "never do such a 'crime' again." It was puzzling since she could have paid, and would gladly do so now if the whole silly matter could be forgotten.

The outfit itself was nothing—an ordinary two-piece white cotton blouse and skirt, "as plain as a napkin," neither expensive nor her style. She doubted that she would ever even have worn it if unapprehended.

Yet, there had been some peculiar and indefinable magnetism about the clothes ever since she had seen them several days before.

Her motive then? "Pure impulse," and "one I could not control no matter how hard I tried."

"Six years ago," she went on, "I came as a domestic to your country, like a lot of other girls. It was then I learned there's no pleasing people. They told me, 'no baby-sitting, just housework.' But Anna was the sitter before long, and the feeder, and the changer too—besides all the other work. I hated it. Naturally I looked to make my situation better. So it made sense to marry Bruno. And I suppose I should say it out, it's a man I never loved—more a 'marriage of convenience.'

"You are wondering if I took things before? No. Never. And probably you don't believe, but it's true. When I did that with the suit it was . . . well, probably that I wanted to test Bruno, to shake him . . . maybe to change that stuffy old guy, and my living with him."

As she poured out the subsequent narrative, it did indeed meander through a lackluster life in a drab and loveless marriage. It had improved her station, but at an awful expense. Their little son, the comfortable home, the handful of interests and scattering of acquaintances hardly compensated for the boredom of days spent in the routine of cooking and shopping. It seemed as if she had leapt from the proverbial frying pan, changing her title of "maid" in fact, but not in substance.

Anna's earlier life was richer: childhood images from Austria recollected a warm family life, brothers, a sister, a father whom she adored but held in awe. He was a professional man, proficient but austere, son of a professor, Grossvater, with whom Anna went to live for several significant years in Berlin. That period with the old man had been restless and lonely, and responsible for her seeking a better future in the New World through an agency that placed girls in jobs with well-to-do families.

I quickly recognized Anna's superior intelligence and good education. An essential integrity of personality, not really hidden by her mechanical scriptlike recitation, lay behind a shell that seemed to be thickest in the area of her time away from home. I was curious why she had left and never returned. I wondered whether anything traumatic had happened, but unable to help her elaborate, ended our interview.

I told her I didn't feel fully satisfied because of her defensive attitude. In these circumstances it was understandable; she was not really free to talk. I should like to mention that in my report, while saying that I found nothing seriously wrong with her mind. However, my preference would be for further examinations and possible treatment if deeper issues were involved.

"And that will be your judgment?" she asked.

I nodded.

Anna stiffened. With a curl of her lip she spit out that I could say whatever I pleased, thanked me perfunctorily, and extended her hand. The other she slapped smartly to her side then spun around and marched through the door to whatever reward or punishment fate and the courts had in store.

I never expected to see or hear from her again, but I was wrong.

*   *   *

Three months intervened between that farewell and her telephone call. She wasted not a syllable nor a breath in detailing how she had "tried therapy" but between her and the social worker recommended by the probation department a "failure of *gemütlichkeit*" made treatment "not much good."

"I must talk with a man, number one, and a physician, number two. I told them so. May I see you?"

*   *   *

It was April 13, 1947, Vienna. Under a crazy quilt comforter Anna looked out on a gray, misty day. Fifteen years old. Fritz and Karen would come. There would be presents. Mother would sing, Father too; then, as usual, from the green velvet-lined violin case he would produce his heirloom and lay it upon the massive mahogany table. She could still see him lather the air with wild, vigorous swings as he resined the bow.

Birthdays meant cakes. With wartime austerities one could always hope, while one tried to accept disappointment maturely.

For sure Father would toast her, slap her back fifteen times then once for luck, and Mother would hug her tearfully. After Fritz and Karen's gifts, and once supper was done, she would be off to the railway station to Berlin where Grossvater would be waiting.

Who knew precisely why, for how long, what it would be like? Would she be homesick, lonely, afraid? What would she do those long daytime hours when he was at the university? Odd, it seemed almost a marriage, their living together.

"How to describe him? Oh, an absent-minded professor I guess, what you call the 'ivory tower type.'

Proud old man. I can still see him with his little white goatee so neatly trimmed, and how he stood every morning before the mirror with the scissors at it."

Anna smiled distantly. She flattened her lips in mild pleasure. Inadvertently stroking her chin, she dreamily brought her legs up under it and for a moment, in reverence to his memory, was silent.

"Wistful?" I asked.

"Nein . . . oh, maybe," she fumbled, "but what was I saying? Nothing important I guess, yet I am somehow uncomfortable. Funny—my pulses are racing. Is the heat in here, Doctor? No? I'm just thinking of Grossvater . . . ah, yes. Ha, there is something only I don't want to talk about it. I suppose I ought. But I really don't want to.

"It's awkward. Oh, damn it! Your silence. It draws a person out so. Yes I've thought of it several times, and I've hoped to forget, but it comes always back—even it was there when I spoke with the social worker. She was so busy writing my answers I kept my secret, but you— hey, why am I shouting? I'm sorry. Anyway, what I guess I'm supposed to tell you today there isn't time. Look at the clock! So, next week, okay?"

And Anna was right. We had no more chance that day. Whatever her confession, it would have to keep.

She rose then, which was usual, but offered to shake hands, which was not. Moreover, in her "good-bye," I heard a hesitation I hadn't before, which probably accounted for my reminding her, significantly even if automatically, of our next appointment.

After she'd gone, for several minutes I pondered that funny formality. Not until the late afternoon was its meaning fully clarified.

"I'm sorry to call when probably you are too busy to talk, so *I* shall. Only just for a minute. When I was there today I forgot to tell you that I can't come in for a while. It's Bruno, er, ah, he feels the treatment takes too long, you see . . . and costs too much. He knows I'll never do it again, and so do I. You can be sure. So I thought we could stop for a while. Is it okay? I'll call you later for another appointment. Really."

To all of which I scrupulously made no reply.

"Look, you can rest easy. I won't do more shoplifts . . . so you needn't worry. Will it be all right? I skip a few sessions, then call, in a month or so. You see Bruno wants to look up North at a business, but I get in touch before, okay? Are you there Doctor?"

"Yes," I replied, "but listen, please. You are right that I am busy just now. Much as I might wish, I can't give you my best attention. I have your promise that discontinuing treatment calls for a discussion, as we originally agreed. Remember?"

She did, and reluctantly acquiesced to another appearance, hastening to assure us both that it would be our last.

The week sped by.

On Thursday, at ten thirty, Anna's hour, my waiting room was empty. Leaving the door ajar to hear her approach, I returned to my desk. Shuffling through the endless paperwork, I sealed, stamped, and stacked a bundle of envelopes in "outgoing," then impatiently reached for an article on dreams.

For the first time Anna was late. Ten whole minutes so far. After fifteen, I knew something was wrong (and reading pointless), so laying the article aside, I gave my thoughts over to the lady and our situation.

"Yes," I mused, "Something is up—she knows it and is struggling over what to do."

When twenty then twenty-five minutes passed I became troubled and doubtful that I'd ever see or hear from her again—until, yes, a clatter of heels, then a flushed and breathless face beaming beneath the familiar bangs and saw-toothed felt cap.

"I'm so sorry to be late. You'll never believe—I got lost on the way. Stupid, eh? After all the times coming. So I tried a short cut and it got all tangled ... so? I suppose you make something of that, eh? Well, it's true enough. Anyway, it's been a very bad week for me. See, I do remember where our meeting ended and my phone call. You were right—it was the shame of it.

"But I've decided to tell you what I've been avoiding. It's better you hear it. Okay? Only don't moralize; promise? So.

"Do you remember how I went to Berlin to live with Grossvater? You were suspecting something about that, eh, well, too bad you couldn't force it out of me then.

"He left me alone very much. Off to the library for some articles he was writing, or the university. I would clean, sweep, do dishes, then one day, shopping at the market, I met Martin—tall, dignified, professional looking, twice my age for sure. *Himmel!* Funny it never occurred to me it could be a father image. Anyway, how it happened I couldn't say but gradually we sought each other out and it seemed impossible to resist.

"Skip details. I got pregnant. And what did I know of such things? Sure he was married. That felt part of the excitement.

"He was frightened too, worried sick, yet still soli-

citous and responsible. I had to trust him, and he said
he would see it through however it had to be. So I tried
not to worry just then.

" 'Hot baths,' he told me. 'Sit in them.' I did, but,
well, they didn't. And 'ride horseback'—which also
didn't. I was pregnant good and no doubt. Seventeen.
And going to have a baby. Then what excitement there
was turned pure fear.

" 'Of course, Martin, I'll keep it a secret. No, never.
Not to a living soul, absolutely,' I promised, when he
spoke of his doctor friend. And I asked over and over
was he sure, sure, sure that everything would be all
right. And I was reassured some, but when I heard that
actual, awful word 'abortion,' then some kind of crying,
shaking, hysterical attack came with guilty nightmares.
Worse because I could tell that Martin, too, beneath the
calm was more frightened than I.

"Isn't it silly? I had to be a support for him so that
he could support me back.

"I told my grandfather an easy lie. I would pass the
weekend with Karen. He was so distracted he hardly
heard. And when Martin came I was waiting, my little
handbag stuffed with slippers and a toothbrush. How
little idea I had.

"I remember climbing into his Mercedes. What
caught my eye—a crack in the leather upholstery. It
looked vulgar. I cranked the seat way back for more
room—like I was already nine months pregnant instead
of three. And what a section we drove through—slums.

"Did you ever have an experience, a happening,
and notice how crazy it is, little insignificant objects become details? We drove through areas I had never
dreamt existed, dark, miserable. I saw bricks in build-

ings. Bricks! Some seemed etched with tiny animal figures, little baby animals.

"When we stopped at a traffic light I saw a house number, '17,' an omen sure, my exact age. And I studied the haloes of street lamps as if they were misty angels. Even I prayed at them. Crazy.

"I suppose we grasp such foolish straws so not to think of something else more awful—like a condemned on his way to the cyanide room studying the corridor walls or the warden's shoes.

"Who knows?"

Anna shifted her position. For the first time she lit a cigarette. Smoke curled out around her nostrils. For a second she stared at the wall, sucked deeply, then tried to push herself way back in the chair, her gestures implying a reliving of that fateful day—and retroactively fortifying herself for it.

"It was dreary. The city was quiet. We got out at a shabby old storefront. Four steps led to a huge door with a brass knocker run through the tongue of a gargoyle. Look what you notice.

"Martin spoke just one word, high-pitched and nervous, 'Come,' and he knocked three times before the door opened. More knocks from my heart against my chest. I thought it would burst.

"Abortion. *Mein Gott!* What have I done? What am I doing here? What is going to happen?

"I was so frightened I really thought to die, then, 'Upstairs?' 'Yes, of course I can walk,' and Martin put a shaky hand under my elbow, trying to calm me with comments about the construction of the building, its age, and how it would last another three hundred years.

"Whom is he fooling? I should care about that structure, its life? What about me, and mine—and its?

"And then, there it all was, what somehow even my ignorance knew enough to predict. The light, the table, the green moth-eaten blinds, the instruments. And a musty, dusty smell like a grave.

"And I knew I should want to scream and scream, and I knew and I knew, and I knew that *he*, that damned, big, no-face, monster-man no one, would ask, 'Will you cry out?'

"And I knew my honesty would say, 'I think, sir, I may,' and that he, clucking, 'We musn't,' would reach behind him—something white and cotton. And I felt, my God, if he tries to put that into my mouth, to stuff it in, it won't fit. But bit by bit he wedged it, so I would burst—and in. Then a second piece. Oh, no. 'Done in a minute.' Oooh, can I breathe?"

Anna fell silent, drained. An eternity passed, then another. Goosebumps rose on her arms (and mine).

To my question whether she understood what she had just experienced she nodded, "Yes," muttering, "How clear. My God, how simple! Oh, how very, very simple, and how it all fits together.

"But please give me just a minute more," glancing at the clock, "I don't think I ever told you how Karen was a key in the whole story."

"A key?"

"Yes."

"You know she is my friend for a very long time. We came together to this country. Every Saturday we met to play cards, to kibbitz. Her I liked best in the whole group. She married a shoe salesman. From the Black Forest. A kind man. But they couldn't have a baby. Ten years they tried and then, all of a sudden, pregnant.

"I was as happy as she was. Maybe more, but, well it wasn't to be. Just three months then she miscarried. For weeks she cried and would see no one, even me, until that Saturday of the shoplift, so I told Bruno I'd be gone until five but I'd call.

"It was a gray, chilly day. When I got to her home I felt uneasy somehow, I rang, but no one answered. I knocked and waited. It was a chance to reflect and I found myself in a 'flashback'—the steps, the door, the bricks in the building, all had a familiar but funny feeling—like everything happened before.

"So, it was only to wait. Then I think, 'She can't be far: I'll shop and come back in an hour.' Why not? It felt good to move away, somehow."

"It was then that you went to Marshall's?" I asked, excited.

"Ja, I went to Marshall's, where it happened, the shoplifts."

"And Karen was three-months pregnant, *three months*," I said. "She lost her child, 'aborted,' and you were going to comfort her?"

"Just so," Anna replied.

As I started to phrase a question pointing out the identical length of her pregnancy, Anna upstaged me with the reply, "Three months was also just as long as I had been. And the two pieces of cotton—the suit, the towels. Just to do—the bag—oh *mein gott!*"

With an unusual and precipitous clarity, the whole story fell into place—the pregnancy, her guilt over it, the abortion—those two cotton towels and the little satchel—short shrift by her grandfather—all triggered by a visit to the Karen of her childhood, following her abortion. Even Anna's compulsion to rework the saga with a male doctor, rather than the female, nonmedical social worker.

It locked and welded itself into a compact explanation that left no room for doubt that her "crime" had been an obligatory fuguelike repetition over which she could have exerted virtually no permanent control.

Indeed, Anna saw along with me how she had for half her life been like a latter-day Canterville ghost doomed to re-enact to its satisfaction a personal vignette with a cast of different characters, new scenes and settings, and a later date, but with "the same basic plot." She experienced enormous relief with near hysterical laughter and copious tears. When composed, she agreed to work through another couple of weeks to drive an extra silver spike through the phantom's ectoplasmic heart.

Only then was it fitting that she yield to her husband's pressures to move north in pursuit of a new business opportunity—despite my unspoken wish that we continue. So (whimsically savoring without comment that she and I had labored exactly nine months together to deliver her of her burden), I discharged her from my care, a little unfulfilled, but content in the conviction that she ought never need be such a thief again.

4
The Philadelphia Lawyer

It had been raining hard all day. An unexpected storm that made the freeway dangerously slick was flooding local streets and turning the hilly approach to my office into a river. Troubled gray skies portended more yet to come. Gusts of wind spit sprays against the louvered windows, squeezing enough through to pool on the sill and trickle down the wall.

Such wild weather was time to be home by a fire, not wondering if one's next appointment would appear. However, even minutes are precious at times, so I had no choice but to sit and wait. Across the room, as the tiny shadows coalesced into a drop, a leak reminded me how many tears had welled and fallen in this place—and how many storms had raged outside and in it.

The lights flickered, and I thought it best to check the answering service before a power failure cut us off.

"Any messages?" I asked.

"Two, Doctor. We've tried to reach you. There must be trouble on your line."

"I guess. What have you got?"

"A cancellation by Mrs. Smith; she can't start her car. And a fellow on the phone now. Can you talk to him?"

The gentleman was in luck. The hour just freed became his. Despite total unfamiliarity with his surroundings and the weather, he was easily directed to my office and within minutes stood at the door.

"How do you do, Doctor?" he began slowly. "I found your name in the Yellow Pages, and I really appreciate your seeing me."

A refined little man, whose elocution and appearance bespoke elegance, he delicately shook the moisture from the transparent slicker he wore to keep his costly, tailored, oxford-gray suit dry.

"I'm a lawyer by trade, yet I know something of your profession, too. I've read about fugues and multiple personalities—not that I'd have thought they'd apply to me. I'm from Philadelphia and I'm certain I'm not crazy. At least I don't think ... yet if I were to defend my actions I'd have to say I'm going through some kind of 'temporary insanity,' which is the reason I called."

The blunt but anguished quality of his manner stimulated an unusually strong urge to hear his story. And as he spun it out I was aware that the storm, the gathering darkness, the circumstances of his visit—all reminded me of a Conan Doyle plot, which impression was in no way diminished as the mystery and suspense began to mount.

"I'm thirty-four, married, with three children, two girls and a boy. I love my wife. Please understand that. We've been married since I was a sophomore at Yale, and we do get along, that is, as well as anyone. At least I always thought so. Yet, here I am in a strange city, thousands of miles from home, living an utterly ridiculous lie with another woman, as if I were acting a movie part in the most trite Hollywood tradition—*only* it's really happening!

"Let me tell you ... how ... what."

Running his fingers through his hair for an instant, he held his head in both hands. A stiffled sob struggled past his tightened facial muscles until, noticing some kleenex, he plucked a couple of tissues swiftly from the dispenser, blew his nose hard, and looked at me through red-rimmed eyes.

Still fighting for composure, he muttered, "I see compassion on your ceiling. It's moved to tears of its own with my plight—look there [pointing to the leak]. But I'm not a punster and you need facts, I know. Here's a thumbnail of it.

"I do corporate work. It's not unusual to be on the road a week, or more. I am, by most standards, successful. I own my own home—stocks, some bonds, money in the bank—belong to Kiwanis and the Temple, a veritable pillar in our community. I'd say my kids are happy. And that my wife loves me. We vacation together and enjoy it. And, I've never, never, never had an affair or a close tie ... with ... anyone in the fourteen years we've been together. Until, until, oh God, this is crazy! I got a phone call from an old classmate—an old, old girlfriend I hadn't seen since college. Out of the blue, on a sabbatical of some kind, 'Just passing through Philadelphia. So can't we get together to say hello to each other—and reminisce?' she coaxed.

"And like some kind of automaton, I met her, had a couple of drinks, lied to my wife that a sudden business trip had come up, and here I am, half loving it, half hating myself, dazed and guilty one minute, then exhilarated beyond reason the next."

A long silence suggested that the lawyer had rested his case.

Into the vacuum my desk clock hurtled its periodic, mechanical "klunk," and our synchronous breathing was counterpointed to the rain. I could hear the silk oak outside groan and sway as the wind, whistling through, combed, raked, then silvered the fernlike leaves while it twisted them backside to.

What a temptation to speak some words of comfort or ask for clarification, embellishment. How cruel it seemed for me to bide my time. But like an artist, I was determined to play my silence with purpose and precision. I needed, imperatively, to hear his very next spontaneous associations, without directing him or contaminating them, even by spoken compassion.

Few people tolerate such silence long and in a minute my patience was rewarded.

"You're after more background, heh?" he asked, breaking it. "Okay, I'll fill you in.

"My real mother died when I was very young. Oh, I'd say five or six—it's hazy. I hardly knew her. 'Presumed to have perished' in a nightclub fire, they said. Maybe you recall it, 'The Mango Grove?' But you know, positive identification was never established; my father—he's a lawyer, too—he remarried ... his secretary.

"I'm an only child, high-strung, bright, I guess, a nail biter until recently and a bed wetter up to thirteen. That's most of it . . . until just two weeks ago, *this*. And it is literally driving me out of my mind. Can you help me, Doctor? I must resolve my lunacy within the next forty-eight hours. Do I simply return to my wife, my kids, my law practice, and the old life, or do I abandon them and run off with Sally? Believe me, even as I hear what sounds so lopsided a conflict, I must impress upon you how torn I am. Intellectual good sense hasn't got it emotionally. I could forsake all for some insane reason. I know right from wrong, but my head and my heart are in separate directions. Can you help me?"

The man seated across from my desk was now stripped of his defenses. Naked and vulnerable, he had reached a pitch of anxious desperation. For all his degrees, courtroom experience, and jurisprudence, his judgment had been reduced to that of a child, a frightened, whimpering, petitioning, five-year-old. And, as I heard myself think that thought, subvocally I enunciated 'child,' then almost automatically I repeated it one more time but ever so slightly aloud.

"A child."

"What?" said my startled listener.

"I said 'a child.' Yes, 'a child.' "

"Well, I guess I am one. Or, at least, I'm acting like one. Is that what you mean? I thought it too, only that doesn't help me resolve anything. Sure it's behaving like one—like a five-year-old. But, what in God's world am I to do, even so?"

"With the rest of your life, I won't tell you," I replied. "But for the next little bit of it, say precisely what you're thinking even if it seems to make no sense.

Whatever, ever, ever enters your head, freely, and all of it, now. Please."

The lawyer looked at me as if I had lost my reason, then softly agreed. "All right. You have some motive . . . My mother comes to mind, somehow. My mother! It's silly, but, all right, I'll tell you. Isn't that stupid? I . . . don't believe she's dead. I never have. I didn't go to her funeral, and, anyway, they weren't positively sure that she was the one in the fire. Oh, I know she's really dead, legally and all, but that's the funny idea that came back just then. When you said 'child,' that's what flashed across my mind. You know, Doctor, I even used to think that one day I might get a phone call from someone I hardly remembered, and it would be my mother—back, to take me away with her and, and, and. . . ."

The Philadelphia lawyer and I looked at each other. Should I remind him that he was a five-year-old when his mother perished and, that he had accused himself of behaving like one, quite literally in his next breath? Ought I interpret Sally as the phoenix who sprang up in the desert of his unfulfilled yearnings? I had need to do neither. Yes, I caught on an instant before him, but his insight was racing up and abreast of mine and looked just then as if it had gone past. He was first to laugh, then I, then we both laughed together. When I could manage it, I asked if he had fully understood the significance of his associations and what they meant to me.

In reply, a wave of tranquility loosened his scalp, relaxed his face, allowed his head to sink into his ribs, his tailored shoulders to slump, and his pelvis to tilt into a position of comfort. He looked at me silently an instant, then said, simply, "Thanks."

That Christmas I received a very large and lovely card with a family photograph of two girls, a boy, a pretty woman, and my legal friend smiling serenely, all posed above the inscription, "The five-year-old Philadelphia Lawyer."

On Accidents

Most accidents don't simply happen. We contribute to them. The evidence is there, in one form or another. I didn't always know that.

Years before my analytic training I was obliged to ride a train from Boston down to Florida. Late to board, I found a solitary seat still vacant in the coach. I slipped into it silently and looking straight ahead quickly began to read my book, in hopes of avoiding entrapment in some boring conversation.

Unfortunately the passenger on my left had taken notice. She began to chat and wouldn't stop. My answers were as curt as I could manage, yet she assailed me with the details of her trip, a pilgrimmage to the Mother Church of Christian Science. Replenished in her faith, she had devised a strategy to save my soul right on that train.

I got lectured to along the whole Atlantic seaboard. How men's illnesses and accidents occur. Bad faith— which sound religious practice might fend off. Endlessly through Worcester, New York City, Jersey, and beyond she had me pinioned. I parried her attack as best I could, until at "Philly" my brotherly love gave out, and despite my firmest resolutions, I fought with passion against everything she said, through Washington, Virginia, Miami Beach.

Years later I reflected: Had I contributed to that debacle? Did I set it up arriving there so late? Would smarter guys have gone off to the smoker? Or lesser masochists cried, "Shut up and let me be!"? Or slapped her face—to demonstrate one "accident" she'd not avoided, in spite of all her faith?

Who's to say? But older now, more experienced, and maybe wiser, I'm not so quick to disregard ideas. And I'm somewhat closer to her line of propaganda— telling tales as if to wield her sword. No, not to champion religious dogma, but rather to reveal my analytic view. Perhaps this group of clinical examples will describe it. Let the reader hear the facts, then judge himself.

5

The Boston Strangler

At precisely three o'clock I went to have a look. It was very hot outside. Shimmering lines of heat were wiggling the contours of the blacktop surface in little sinusoidal waves.

No one was there.

Humid and heavy, the air was hard to breathe. Browning patches on the lawn evidenced how quickly the morning watering had dried up and left the greenery to parch, then wilt and die. Smog was everywhere. August in the San Fernando Valley. There'd be no relief from nature yet for weeks.

That afternoon the elements held sway, uncontested. Every resident who owned one, all at once, had put his cooler on. Result: a power failure. Even my tiny office perched on its hill, so much a wind sock set to capture breezes blown from anywhere, and with its mottled shade beneath an ancient walnut and a tall silk oak, even it became a steam bath, instantly.

I should have to tell as much to Mrs. Culp as soon as she arrived, then offer her an alternate appointment if she wished. In temperatures like these to try to concentrate seemed foolishly ambitious.

So I sat on the wall and waited, thinking it too bad to start a therapy this way. Appropriate or not, I feared the lady might feel rejected if I sent her away—a lot of folks are extra-sensitive. But just then a noisy, orange-yellow, boxy taxicab pulled up to the front gate and stopped. Its driver quickly ran around and opened the rear door.

From my vantage point I couldn't see the passenger—not yet. That is, at least not all of her. I was to meet that woman seriatim, and, in retrospect, the most important parts in order of significance—feet first. A strange sight to be sure. Slowly, to the rhythm of the engine knocks, with serpentine undulations, there emerged a stockinged, knee-length plaster cast—and then the rest of Mrs. Culp—the full 200 pounds.

I strolled up to the cab and, offering my hand, I introduced myself, silently reflecting all the while how much her features reminded me of edibles. Her face was large and round—a bowl of cream of wheat decorated with two black raisin-eyes; lipstick cherry red encircled her milk-white teeth.

"I'm Frances Culp," she wheezed, then reaching back, she accepted the aluminum crutches the driver fed to her and tucked them underneath her wings.

I made my little speech about the heat but, when deep furrows creased her brow, I added that if she preferred, I'd tough it out. I'd leave the choice to her. Without a blink she said, "Let's carry on!"

So, slowly, together, we started down the twenty yards to where we'd work. Hobbling uncertainly, she picked her way as far as the three broad wooden stairs. These she negotiated like a stroboscopic film. Each aspect of that minitrip she studied first, rehearsed, then acted out until she'd gained the threshold of the door, whereat she pivoted, passed through, then paused before the chair. Turning, she clapped the crutches together, allowed the cast to slide forward along the carpet and her bulk to sink into the seat.

She looked at me and I looked back.

From the cleavage of her peasant blouse Mrs. Culp produced a daintily embroidered handkerchief. With it she fanned her face, breathing fast and shallowly, then smiling nicely said, "Yes, it is warm, but if I steamed off five, ten pounds here in your sauna it wouldn't do me harm. Do you agree?"

Her problem? Losing weight. It was affecting everything—her heart, her lungs, and even, come to think of it, that's how she'd wrenched her knee. A freaky accident. She blushed; was she obliged to talk of that?

I gestured, "Please," to which the following unfolded, piece by piece.

In April of that year her family had been transferred to the Los Angeles branch of the firm for which her husband worked—a feather in his cap, to be selected from such an elite group, and sent to blaze the trail for later, larger moves. It scared them though to realize how much his whole career might hinge on his success.

The relocation brought them into contact with all new personnel, which made it natural enough for Mr. Culp to ask his wife to plan a dinner party, particularly since she was a "super chef." What better way to meet the crew than through a gourmet feast? The guest list would include the boss, the vice-president, the major sales reps, and their wives—a bunch of V.I.P.'s. Oh yes, she had her work cut out, but cooking was good fun and she was used to it.

The party day was typical for June. Cool early morning fog obscured the distant hills. Eager to begin, Mrs. Culp dressed, maneuvered her kids to school, double-checked with the baby-sitter to be sure about their rendezvous, then found her shopping list. Leaving her husband shaving, she was off to market before either he or much of the city had fully waked.

Uncrowded check-out lines sped her through the store; back before ten, within an hour she had diced the peppers, pimentos, garlic, olives, and cukes, and added them to a tomato base for cold gazpacho soup. By noontime, well ahead of schedule, it was chilling in the huge tureen beside the marinade and salad in the fridge.

Then, bustling through the house she collected all the scattered dishes, glasses, ash trays, and silverware, and set them in the washer. Humming happily, she straightened, dusted, swept, and vacuumed; put towels in the guest bath; set a magazine at angles on the coffee table (to look read); made a final check; and, feeling she had earned it, took her lunch.

At one, she added her dirty dishes to the load already in the machine, clamped and ran it, then she snipped twelve roses from behind the garage. These she placed in vases all around the room. Next she portioned out the nuts, fruits, and chocolates in their trays and laid them here and there. But something was still missing. She went back and cut a bunch of little fragrant yellow blossoms high up on their stalks, and mixing them with fern, floated them in a cut-glass centerpiece. She stood back and smiled, quite pleased with the effect.

Placemats, napkins, flatware, everything all set and only three fifteen. She had at least a precious hour to sit, fix a drink, and contemplate, to smoke just one cigarette. Why not? She'd earned that too.

Parties were always fun. Mrs. Culp knew she had a flair for entertaining. The secret of putting people at their ease was feeding them well and caring about the way in which you did it. She enjoyed serving, helping, offering of herself. Her husband even used to tease her on that point, that they had named her "Frances" for the Saint. St. Francis with his love and care of little animals. She didn't mind. The world would be a better place if everybody followed her philosophy, the golden rule: to love thy neighbor as thyself.

She'd always been like that, even as a youngster. Yes. What a pretty planet we would have if charity and grace were practiced as they were preached. Ah, me! One sip of alcohol and there she was, reflective, maudlin, reminiscent. That was no mood to wallow in. Frances! Shuck it off. Get rid of it. Right now, she told herself.

* * *

And as her narrative flowed on, I interjected nothing more than grunts, and few of those. Her story had its lilt. I chose to let it be, admiring both her power

of description and her way with words. They left me
feeling I could literally follow every move, the
shopping, cleaning, cooking. Every part became so
visual. I saw it totally—that is, except one tiny area,
when in contrast to the rest she paused to introspect and
somehow saddened over something, something which
she didn't say. Something she avoided elaborating.
Why? And what? I didn't have an inkling.

*   *   *

Surreptitiously the early haze had blown away.
The sky was brilliant blue and clear, and, in his
downward arc, old Sol began to beat directly on the
city's western face. The adobe walls of Spanish homes,
the sides of newer high rise structures, the distant
mountains, all reflected back his hot intensity.

From her kitchen window, Mrs. Culp stood
pensively a moment watching the Coast Bank Building.
One hundred mirrors, reddened by the sun, seemed
ablaze. It was as if behind their glass façade a conflagra-
tion burned. She noticed the thermometer on top. It
read 104 degrees! Incredulous, she clucked her tongue.

A stifling evening was in store. How wise to serve
cold soup. But save us ... such a heat!

When her husband sagged in, shirt-sleeved,
sopping wet, and freeway-wilted, she knew at first
glance that he was "spastic." Under pressure Henry had
his way of coming all unglued. His temper flared; he
spoke too fast and thickly, repeated himself and tended
to get flustered and forget. Like the liquor for the
party—rotten luck.

Calmly Frances let him unwind, fixed him a

snack, served him a drink, and even joined in his remonstrances against summers in the West. He kept it up as if it were her fault that in humidity like this their water cooler wasn't worth two pins. Then he reminded her that if this party didn't go his head might roll. Yes, it was critical and he was counting on her help.

All of which managed to undermine her confidence just a tiny bit, to depress her half a notch, without her knowing why. But, shooing him away good-naturedly, she urged him to wash and change then pick the liquor up—there wasn't too much time.

*   *   *

Upstairs, alone, Frances sat a moment as her bathtub filled. Damn! Some fool thing was eating her. A tear slid down her cheek. What was that hollow in her gut, that pressure on her breast? So heavy and so sad. Had Henry got to her? Could she be frightened, choking up at the responsibility? No, that wasn't it. Perhaps the heat or plain fatigue; she'd slept so poorly and had such wild dreams. Or could it be the move? The friends they'd left back East?

Whatever. She spun the spigot round and shut the water off. Slipping into it, she let herself unwind.

The bath left her steaming, certainly no fresher, and impossible to dry. Glimpses at her torso made her vow again to diet—all next week. The fleshy folds retained her body heat. Agh! It wasn't fair to labor so just dressing. The hairspray wouldn't hold it was so damp. Her make-up clumped and floated on her skin, and the dusting powder wouldn't pat or spread. What a nuisance to be fat and try to do one's toilet—let alone in weather of 104 degrees. No, she liked the climate better back in Boston. Thinking that, she heard the doorbell ring.

Frances hastened to the window. Two huge black limousines were parked along the curb. Three couples, one with flowers, stood beneath the arbor at her door. What time was it anyhow? Could she have dozed while relaxing in the tub?

Guests. Too soon. Too early. Was Henry out? Yes, Frances was alone. Upstairs and half-dressed. Ye Gods! Now Frances, fight your panic. Take it slowly. You've got to keep it cool. Carry on!

And saying that she reached out for the garment closest by, her girdle, grabbed it firmly and began to pull at it. But it fought her all the while, until half way up it slid beneath her fingers and snapping like a vicious reptile gripped her round the knees. She watched her thighs begin to scissor, lost her balance, and went down.

Oh Lord! Oh Lord! Of all the things! Who needed this? Were her legs broken? Still no pain, but look. Her knee was cocked into a really crazy angle. Heaven help her; it was out of joint.

Okay Frances. Pull yourself together. The party must go on. There is no other choice. And thinking that, she grasped the dislocated member, shut her eyes, and thrust it back in place.

Incredible! Even more that she survived that evening. Pallid, smiling wanly, drinking to excess to numb the throbbing pain, she managed, until 2 a. m. The last guest barely cleared the driveway when she turned the stopcocks, let it out, and told her husband all.

*   *   *

Despite her protests about housework and her kids, Mrs. Culp was sedated and admitted to an orthopedic ward. Her shattered knee was cased in plaster. Later in that day she heard the baleful news: proper healing called for losing weight. Her body was a heavy pile driver crashing down on that injured joint with every step. Had she ever tried to diet? Could she lose, say fifty pounds that year?

Her response to the doctor's queries was that she would try and see. Most of the gain had been quite recent, since their moving from the East. Maybe half of what he wanted off she'd added since that trip. As to his suggesting something psychological, she had her doubts but kept an open mind. She promised, if he recommended it, to call for an appointment with his friend, an analyst who practiced up the hill.

She did. I had a busy schedule but could meet her later in the week, on Friday at three o'clock.

*   *   *

Following that informative first outpouring, the outline of her past was rather drab. Mundane. Early childhood, schooling, five-and-dime employment, courtship, even marriage and the births of both their kids were routine. Nothing peaked above the clinical horizon; there were few trouble areas within her life.

Friendly, altruistic, happy in the role fate had shaped her into, Mrs. Culp was coping all around. Why not? Secure, because her husband truly loved her (even if his style was somewhat immature), and attentive to the needs of her children, she seemed a lady well-adjusted to the frets and rubs of young adulthood in these times. In fact, my first assessments scored her high in that regard. The only fact about which I had some misgiving was that melancholic spell before the guests arrived. It would warrant further probing. Maybe we could focus back and clarify.

I summed things up then, highlighting all the positives. She had shown a lot of courage and self-sacrifice. Few women could have "carried on" the way she did to see it through. Her relationship with her family really sounded wholesome, yet I had, I said, a question here and there, to shed some light.

That accident—it was really unusual. Was it true, I queried, that life goes flashing past a person's eyes before he falls?

She nodded in agreement, so I asked her what she'd seen. She mumbled something, but appeared annoyed that I should question. When I pushed to learn what reverie she'd entered into in her tub and at that "breather" when she had sat and smoked and had her drink, to my surprise her face grew dark and stormy. The raisins glowed like shining little beads. Across her flat and smoothly contoured forehead a ridge of brow defined itself in sharp relief. She was angry all at once, enraged at me.

What had I said or done I asked her? However, I didn't press. I feared she'd up and run.

Some minutes passed in silence, then, composing her features, she let me see her profile. Gazing through the window, toward the floor, she muttered that she was sorry, and asked me to forgive her. She would try to answer and to "cool it." She'd do her level best to "carry on."

That funny phrase. Again. Was she British? Had she read or heard it said somewhere before? In the story with the girdle did she realize she'd used it several times? At that she shouted, "Gee, you're picayune. You really pounce on silly little nothings. What nit-picking. It's a saying I suppose I use a lot. Big deal! Is this a school? If treatment means I've got to watch each single word I mouth, then let's forget it.

"Oh look, I'm truly sorry. This isn't me at all. I must be overtired. Or it's this heat. Maybe we should have waited for cool weather . . . coming here, this leg. Will you forgive me please? What did you want to know?

"To 'carry on?' That's Henry. He's the culprit. It's his saying. He was based in England during the war.

"Can you believe he's after me to entertain again? And me on crutches, and with this heat? But I'm not playing by the rules. You're right. Okay, there's more. My God, you're clever aren't you? Yes, there's more. Funny that I couldn't spit it out. I feel so guilty. I wasn't mad at you at all—it's me. There was an incident in Boston. Will you forgive my childish outburst, please?"

But as she settled back, familiar engine knocks were heard outside the door. I might have guessed and timed things better. Her taxi had arrived. We'd have to quit, for then.

*   *   *

Should I "forgive" the "childish outburst?" I'd done nothing to provoke it. All her feelings had some other source. This was a vital clue.

Would I forgive it? Her question was tantamount to asking if detectives should forgive the fingerprints they find on weapons. Rest assured. I waited eagerly until we'd meet again.

Generally speaking, I have found it fruitless to remind patients where time interrupted. Too many other things have usually intervened. Good technique focuses attention on whatever surfaces at a given moment, not upon the therapist's curiosity, however strong it may be. When folks do ask me to bring them back to where we left off, I often use a favorite analogy. Progress in therapy, I say, is like a wagon wheel. If one picks any spot on the perimeter, proceeds to the first spoke, and follows it to the hub, it doesn't matter where he starts, or which path he follows; all routes lead to the same core. And so it is if one just speaks his thoughts. That gets us back to where we ought to be.

Mrs. Culp however was an exception. She needed no reminder, no metaphor. Seated at our next encounter she started her narration as if she had been yearning to all week long.

*　　*　　*

Their Boston apartment house was one of that venerable city's least proud accomplishments. Formerly prestigious, the area had run down as ethnic groups encroached upon it. Residing there was bearable because it saved commuting time and costly rents, but outweighing those advantages were the noise and plethora of kids. It was crowded, teeming.

Each family had two or three children, except the folks who shared their landing down the hall. Theirs was a solitary, bashful boy who seldom peeked outdoors. His mother, equally reclusive, was a disappointment to gregarious Mrs. Culp. To live in such proximity yet have no one to "klatch" with, well, that was really frustrating. However, efforts to extend herself toward this "shy" and "wind-blown" woman "cut no ice." She saw her only taking in the milk or putting out the trash.

Mid-April, on a Tuesday evening, Mrs. Culp was bustling through the dinner dishes, while her husband watched his T. V. in the den. From her distance she tuned it out, thalamically reflecting over the preparations for their move—the packing, the good-bye presents, and the party she was catering that week to toast their East Coast friends. Suddenly a scream came through the bedroom wall. At intervals, shouting, the sounds of dishes smashing, and muffled strugglings suggested something awful going on next door.

Frightened, Mrs. Culp ran to her husband who was standing, frozen, listening himself. Together they heard an ambulance siren wailing in the street outside their house. Through the living room window, and seconds later at the front door peephole, Mrs. Culp followed two white-jacketed attendants who mounted the stairs, then entered the adjoining suite. Minutes later, out they came. Oh, what a sight.

Strapped on the stretcher lay the neighbor, thrashing, yanking futilely against restraints. Poor thing. Screeching, cursing, down the steps, around the spiral stairwell, followed by her husband and the child, then gone.

A ghastly spectacle. It haunted Mrs. Culp. She knew it would.

*   *   *

Unresponsive to her husband's urgings, she set up
vigil in the parlor and surveyed every car that came into
their street or left. Midnight found her sitting still.
Finally at one a.m. the neighbor's husband returned.

Leaping to invite him in, to offer of her ample
bosom, she convinced that weary man to stop by, with
the boy. She'd been waiting, she said, hoping she could
serve him something, help out somehow; she had seen
and heard. How awful it had been. Could she fix him
breakfast? Could she please? Or would he join them in
the morning, just that once?

As an answer, talking to some distant purpose, the
neighbor said his wife had "flipped her lid," that she'd
had a first-class nervous breakdown that night. Tried to
choke the boy for some damned foolish reason. More
than likely she'd been drinking. Lucky he could get the
rescue squad to come. It had happened once before in
Jersey. Yes, they took her all the way to County—you
should have heard what she was screeching those ten
full miles. No, it didn't make no sense to him, no way.
In fact, he wondered what possessed him to get married
anyhow to a woman with a kid and "screamin' fits."

*   *   *

His monologue left quite an imprint on her mind.
All that night she didn't shut her eyes one wink.
Tossing, twisting as the antique clock chimed "four,"
she poked her husband into waking, asking if he
thought that she had been remiss.

Poor man (he'd been dreaming of promotions and
L. A.). Wasn't it so? Shouldn't she have pushed herself a

little harder, to extend a helping hand? That sad soul.
Think of it, to try to choke the boy. Just contemplating
the picture, why it gave her the willies. And had he seen
her writhing on the stretcher? Heard those curses? No
one should be left too much alone. Did he agree?

Wearily her husband begged her, "Go to sleep."
She wasn't "Albert Schweitzer." He had work that
morning. So did she. She should concentrate on things
that made more sense. That girl was sick. Forget her.
Besides, there was so much that they had to do the next
day. Was she forgetting the farewell party? And the
shopping and the planning? Did she even know her
menu? Jesus Christ! If she had so much time to offer she
could come down to his office. Plenty of work to keep her
busy. So go to sleep. Okay?

Good thinking. She'd try. At five fifteen, she did.
And all morning long she bustled valiantly—yet the
specter haunted her that day.

She would make amends, if ever that wan creature
returned. Think of it! For an entire year the two families
had lived in such proximity, yet she hardly knew that
woman's name to say "hello." Well, nobody should
have to go neglected. So she'd been married once
before; what could have happened then? And she'd been
drinking—how sad.

Even if her husband teased her, Frances Culp would
"do her Christian thing." She'd keep tabs. Go meet her
properly. Have them in to dinner. Cheer her up. Wasn't
it awful that a mother could attempt to choke her son?
Yes, at least part of such a story must have been sins of
omission. They had no friends at all. No one ever
visited or called. Well, she'd keep tabs. They'd see. One
ought.

That resolution gave her peace of mind, until quite unexpectedly her promise faced its test.

*   *   *

Wednesday, the day before the farewell party and the last chance she had to do the marketing for it, early in the morning Mrs. Culp drove toward a suburb where she felt she got the choicest cuts of meat. At a red light on a corner close to home, there was the neighbor, riding in a cab—apparently she'd been released and let return.

Struggling with her intuitions and an urge to turn around, Frances reasoned that the shopping must be done. But, if she hurried, why, within two hours she could hop across and pay a friendly call.

Hmph! Had they found her normal and discharged her? Was her husband in the cab? She seemed so pale and woe-begone. Best to hurry. She had made a resolution and would keep it. Yes indeed!

As the time slipped by, however, the lady's image gnawed at the fringes of her mind. It built. It grew. Her preoccupation bordered upon frenzy. It was urgent that St. Francis race back home.

Panting on arrival, she trembled, pressing on the neighbor's bell. Upstairs it rang. No response. Nor did her second or her third attempts get answered. Nothing stirred. Mrs. Culp pushed through and climbed up to her flat. At the door she grasped the knocker and then breathlessly began a loud tattoo. No sound. When again there was no reply, she kicked the frame. Was it possible the lady'd gone to do some errands? Or was she showering and thus unable to hear the noise at her door? Sensing these as lame excuses, Frances called the super for his key.

Good Lord!

Her neighbor sat, half-undressed and catatonic, astride her blood-soaked bed. Beside her, on it, lay the boy, his head bashed in.

* * *

The party? Well, it had been scheduled. And her husband urged her to be brave and "carry on." His very words. Anyhow, it wouldn't have helped the little chap to cancel, or his mother, or the husband who had flown the coop just after they had talked the night before. Her guilt? Why it certainly would mellow; she would see. Just heed her husband's words; keep busy. Life goes on.

* * *

Q. E. D. To solve her problem all I needed was to tie together how the second party in L. A. recalled the one in Boston, how the weight which she was gaining was a shield, and how that wistful moment when she sat there weeping and sipping scotch, then in her tub, had been in requiem to honor someone gone—the little lad. And to prove my theorem on accidents and how we shape them, I might point out to her that her guilt had picked the girdle for revenge—when it threw that deadly stranglehold around her legs.

Convincing? No? Not really? I'd have thought it all fell neatly into place. Let's see. . .

Oh, how stupid! I've left out one tiny detail. One which clinches it beyond the faintest doubt. The coroner's report: it read that before the neighbor stove her small son's skull in, to spare him suffering, she'd choked the boy. *She'd strangled him.*

Just as the girdle did.

6

The Boomerang

Mr. Facts.

Just a glance revealed that Victor was an engineer: a thick-necked, powerful, no-nonsense guy who obviously had small use for sentiment, or psychiatric folderol. Not him! He ran on scientific tracks with logic, numbers, pi-squares, and binomials, not shadows in the air or ghosts in some machine.

His features—those craggy brows, the contour of his mouth, the angle of his jaws—were authoritative, strong, like plates from an anatomic text, all perfectly symmetrical. They emphasized his thrust; one felt it when he spoke.

To broadcast his views he overstressed his words, italicizing them, and even when he smiled, his grin retained its leer. It bared his yellow teeth: twin sets of piano keys, wide-arced and double-tiered, flashing constantly.

You picture him? With his graying bristle-top and the stubble on his cheeks, with his yard-wide shoulder spread and barrel-chested girth? He was a panzer tank with inch-thick armored walls, a man who wouldn't dally long without concrete results.

And yet, they'd sent him to consult me because of accidents occurring left and right. They feared his breaking down. I was to talk with him, to pierce his outer crust, then probe his inner parts, all psychologically.

When I asked him to expound, he bellowed back at me that the firm for which he worked had blackmailed him into coming, because of "boomerangs." "Too many just for chance," he cried. "They got some nutty thought *I'm* sabotaging *me*. Myself! I don't believe in masochistic crap. I'm 'captain of my fate and master of my soul.' It's me who calls the shots, and never the reverse.

"Look. I'm an engineer. I dig holes in the ground. *I* tell men what to do. They got me all screwed up. My bag is basic stuff, like mass and gravity. And yet, to speak the gospel truth, my luck's been running bad.

"See this? I broke my wrist. I slipped on somethin' slick, an oil spot on the deck. That was the final straw. There's not much more to tell. Now you can read your script, but skip the double talk an' I'll cooperate."

My thoughts I kept within, since I could translate his. Their message clearly read if I stepped in his den he'd gladly chew me up. If I made one false move we'd blow to smithereens, the therapy and me. I had to poke around and find some tiny chink. Perhaps approach him through his eyes; they looked most sensitive.

To them I softly said, "They got you quite annoyed by sending you up here. You know they phoned me, too, and gave me a report. You've had a lot of lumps. That much is surely true. It could be they're all flukes. Let's hear the evidence."

He stepped right on my lines. "To see if *I* hate *me*? No way. My middle name is *Wynn*, and that's no accident. I picked it out myself. Uh uh. This busted bone's a goof. It cost 300 bucks to get this plaster cast. Christ! What sense would it make to stick myself like that. Besides, I'll ask it to you straight. Don't accidents occur to you psychiatrists? You ever break a bone or get a razor cut?"

To duck that cannon ball I laughed, "I'm sure at times we do," as Victor pressed his point.

"Okay, then you agree. So why look deeper down? Am I 'neurotic,' Doc?"

Again I gentled him, "I couldn't say, not yet. For that I'd need your help."

He smiled his leer and said, "Whatever help you want, but skip the page on wrists. You know, I saw a movie once about a masochist. That guy was strictly nuts. You going to try to prove that I'm as weird as him?"

To which I simply shrugged, "I'm neutral, jokes aside. I'll play it as it lies. Suppose you fill me in on your biography?"

"Great. Anything you need. Just shoot the questions, Doc. I got no crimes to hide. Go on. Just poke away. Which parts you wanna hear?"

To answer him I said, "Well, as a rule of thumb, what you'd least care to tell. That speeds the process up. Whatever surfaces, whichever thoughts emerge; don't try to sort them out."

"Go where it goes?" he asked. "Okay, that sounds like fun. Let's start with accidents. The first time I got hurt, way back in '42. My job was checking valves and logging my results. I'd write my figures down then move the hell on out. Know why? 'Cause overhead were pipes filled with this caustic stuff. A guy could get blown up if they should ever burst.

"Well, following routine, one day I turned the bend, and there it was, a leak. It burned me good right here and creased my scalp. See this?

"It could'a been much worse, a *real big* accident. So how does that come through? I mean was that my fault? Did I have a hand in it or set it up somehow? I mean, I didn't hang those pipes or fill 'em with that stuff, or nail that goddam chart beneath them on that wall, or schedule rounds I made. I *followed orders*, Doc. I was quite blameless, no?"

He sat and glared at me.

"You analyze that, Doc? That masochistic, huh? I'd say that time was chance. What's your computer read?"

I waited then I asked, "Where was it that you worked?"

"In an explosives plant," he roared. "I volunteered of course. I wasn't scared one bit. I love that kind of thing. I like to risk my neck."

Italics filled the air. I asked him nevertheless, if he would be so kind to say that last again. Then I ran it through twice more, until I was sure he'd heard.

7

Three Strikes, You're Out

Yes, Jeanie was a pixie.

But even pixies can have problems. Fresh, petite, and charmingly impractical, she became a playful melody to Levin's solemn counterpoint the day she said, "I do."

With marriage, Levin's bachelor's nest high in the hospital tower, under the bells, became inadequate. Some floors below, a high-ceilinged, three-room suite lay vacant, mouldering. True it had two major flaws: the access through an ancient water-powered elevator and its kitchen area, shared by the entire landing. However, spacious and furnished (Jeanie called the decor "Early Transylvanian"), it certainly would do for the two young newlyweds.

Lev cornered Dr. Aster, the hospital administrator. He huffed and puffed about seniority and setting precedents, but then finally yielding, he made arrangements with the housekeeper for their moving in over the weekend of the Fourth. The path was now cleared for married life.

Jeanie saw it all through a kaleidoscope: her distaff involvement in the residency training program proved a dizzying, unique experience. New words, new rules, new faces. Frequently she couldn't tell, except for the clutch of keys around their middles, who were the employees, who the patients. That scared her some.

Unsure of what to say and how to act with whom, bewildered by conflicting wisdoms from a dozen varied authorities, she felt beset—ever questioning how personal to be, how cautious, how discreet, and who, if anybody, on the grounds was prone to violence.

Besides, the East was so damned "Eastern," with its humid, sultry days and its climate changing instantly. Imagine, in July it rained. How unthinkable to hold a picnic in an auditorium as torrents poured outside. She wrote that to her friends.

Yet Jeanie did adapt. She soon grew popular with everyone, men and women alike. Her unspoken charisma moved the former to father and protect, the latter to reach out helpfully. To neither did she pose a threat.

*   *   *

Of the literally scores that Jeanie met, she attained greatest familiarity with the guys sharing their floor: Rod, the handsome prima donna who'd been altar-bound but got cold feet; Rafe, ungainly Rafe, who seldom dated girls; and Ned who claimed to have a fiancée in England, whom he'd marry "bye and bye."

She concentrated her activities on ways to make things easier for Levin. He worked like an Olympic athlete. Gone from early morning, all day long he ran around his wards solving patients' problems, attending conferences, doing psychotherapy, and then, four evenings out of five, he participated in the clinic, seminars, and journal club—away until the tower chimes quit tolling fifteen minute intervals. Past ten o'clock.

Jeanie tidied, dusted bric-a-brac, vacuumed the faded thinning carpet until the fibers showed, and straightened browning photographs of mutton-chopped and bearded, long-gone superintendents. Frequently she crawled wearily, alone, into their old iron-frame double bed, a little wistful, to think and rest until her hubby came.

Jeanie's routine started with the breakfast dishes and her stereo. Then she'd smoke at coffee, sit, and read. Novels and magazines led to pocketbooks about romance, until she dipped her pretty little toes into the tempting waters of psychiatry: *A Mind that Found Itself, The Lust for Life, The Fifty Minute Hour*, then Adler, Jung, Horney, and Freud, all at once. Whenever there was a chance she bull-sessioned with the guys who kept popping in and out. She listened retentively, a sponge sucking up and holding in the wisdom of their words.

Rafe paid tribute just in stopping by. Ned once made a pass at her, and Rod, well, Rod gave her the ultimate compliment. He was jealous that Levin got to Jeanie before he did. He vowed to find her twin.

Jeanie adored Levin. She loved the universe to which he'd introduced her. His was an entirely new field of meaningful endeavor. Being in it brought a sense of validation, of purpose. She thrilled to realize that married now, and more articulate, she was coming to appreciate her intuitions. She could hear the whispers from her chromosomes telling her all kinds of perquisites of being human, feminine. How exciting to learn to classify and name such feelings.

Until something spoiled it. Jeanie suddenly turned blue, nostalgic, inconsolable, so immutably that Levin, who was my student, asked if I'd consult with her to see what might be done to bring his Trilby back to him, to mute those distant wailing oboe notes that lured her from his reach.

*   *   *

At our initial meeting Jeanie poured her troubles out. Sensitive creature. How easily rejected.

Afraid to burden Levin with her woes, to tarnish his career, she nobly kept locked up inside herself how much she missed her folks, her childhood haunts, the western flora and the surf, her lifelong chums, and how she struggled with dependency and loneliness, then lately, with fantasies of harm to herself.

She asked if I could squeeze her in.

*   *   *

Early September, just after Labor Day, her formal therapy began. She lay on my couch, her little ankles crossed, her tiny hands folded as in prayer upon her midsection, as she gradually fleshed out the framework of her past. Every hour spelled some progress, and inched us upward slightly in our climb to fresher airs.

Leaves changed color, dried, and brittled. Frosts began to greet the morning light. The nights lengthened and grew crisper, while precipitation turned from rain to sleet and hail. Freezes locked an icy winter into place, until one little thaw enticed the groundhog out to find his shadow. He brought crocuses, then lilacs, bright spring tulips, and new buds to trees left naked months before.

How many hours of therapy? A year of it had passed.

In drawing lots to settle their vacation, Levin won first pick. He and Jeanie chose July to bolt up north to Canada to sun and swim. But her husband warned her, she must clear with me to get herself "excused."

Smiling prettily she listened, just a whit impatient, as I intoned about dependency and "acting out" and cautioned her how relationships build surreptitiously, how our sessions had established a rhythm she was apt to miss. I asked her to be thoughtful and observant, wished her well, and scheduled her return.

Jeanie pooh-poohed my concerns. She taunted me about "transference reactions" and laughingly exempted herself from such "Hollywoodisms." She anticipated neither fidgets nor the blues. Hadn't we picked the bones of that subject and hung them out to dry? Besides one month was just an eye-blink. Anyhow, she'd managed without doctors all her life.

So, Levin borrowed fifty dollars from provident

Rafe and a tent from Rod, then packed their gear while Jeanie fussed with sandwiches. Together they mapped their route to Crystal Lake. Minutes later, close to nine a.m. they "hit the Pike." Jeanie shook her head from side to side and clucked her tongue. Laughingly she jabbed her hero's ribs.

"Lev, you won't believe this, but I think I've 'acted out.' Guess what. I didn't bring a bathing suit; that's what. Sweetheart, could we stop at Simpson's? They'll be open. I'll hop in and grab one ... off the rack ... ten minutes. Time me. Please?"

And Jeanie opened Simpson's huge glass door to race on through.

Look out!

Her sandal and her toe slipped underneath the door. Ouch! It bled profusely, necessitating an inch of stitchwork—at the hospital emergency (of course), where Levin held her hand and rolled his head, and kept his mouth shut to avoid interpretations which she didn't need to rub in what she'd done.

Well, they were young. They both healed quickly and salvaged some vacation anyhow. They came back full of bounce and vigor, ripe for tackling all the chores that lay ahead: another year of residency training, and for Jeanie, further work at psychotherapy.

It too passed.

Pumpkins, turkey, Santa, Easter bunnies, Mayday. Her analysis went plunging deeper than before. With her oboes we were blending sad bassoons. We were still digging at the roots of her depression when vacation time came around once more.

Was there need to preach anew my sermon? "No sir." Jeanie remembered and assured me there was not.

She had bought a blue bikini. It was already tucked up in her suitcase. And she promised to wear sneakers, to be extra cautious. No more "acting out," I'd see. Dependency and medical attention—two dead issues, long since buried.

In the morning, at the hour of their departure, Levin whistled as he took her by the hand. He snapped her seat belt on himself, to play it safe. Then he slammed the door.

Oh no!

Jeanie left her finger sticking out. On the rim. God what a goof! Struck by lightning twice instead of once. Sound like classic accident proneness?

Well, best laid plans of mice and men. . .

Back to the emergency again. Once more her digits got sewn up. Levin couldn't resist a dash of sauce to spice his healing balm. So, she'd got herself right back to doctors after all. "Okay. Remember. Tell it to your 'shrink' when we return."

Jeanie did. Together we were able with that anecdote to drop to depths that really plumbed her core—orality and its profound attachments and her infant needs to stay "umbilicated" to the source, to where anxiety was spawned. We glimpsed into the furnaces of life; she saw the molten metals. Or so I thought, until we came to test our theory once a-gain.

Vacation time.

Older, wiser, more sophisticated Jeanie (still a pixie) guaranteed that she would make it all the way. Why not? And sailing northward toward the border, just one hundred miles to go, toes and fingers still intact, suddenly lightning struck again.

Jeanie's sunny face grew cloudy ... and ... she asked if Lev ... would mind ... stopping ... the car. One final time.

How come?

Huge salt tears gushed down her cheeks. "Here," she urged him. "Put your finger on this thing inside my mouth. Feel that?"

Levin did and found a stony tumor mass, hanging, growing out of her hard palate—really there. Well, this time he was pretty scared himself. So, he sped back to the city, to our ear, nose, and throat consultant to the staff.

Know what the expert said?

"Go back on your vacation, muttonheads. Levin, didn't you ever see a torus palatinus? Jeanie, that's a normal variation. Been there in your mouth since you were born."

8
Sonya and the Monster

Of all psychiatric treatments, the most awesome is classical psychoanalysis. For years its participants, five hours a week, lie upon the doctor's couch. There, according to the rule, they must allow themselves to "free-associate," to learn to think aloud.

In time, with skill, and if he's fortunate, the therapist gradually assumes a ghostly congruence with figures from his patient's past. The analysis of that relationship as seen by light of day, through adult eyes, gives options where before there were none, affording a chance for change and even "cure."

The process is the best approach to date to recalibrate one's childhood foibles, set the record straight, and to rethink one's infant days, yet it is expensive, long, frustrating, painful, and replete with imperfections.

And so it isn't a disgrace to share with students of the art an instance where the effort failed. Indeed, omitting this account would violate the canons of good teaching, for in reporting *Sonya* I shall show, I hope, that I had operated well, with good technique, poise, and wisdom. Still, in the end, my patient exercised his choice to interrupt the task half-done, as any human has his right to do, to terminate without his doctor's blessing, and in a way that left me with the deepest of regrets, to be sure.

Karel.

He was among the meanest, sickest, brightest "birds" I'd every met. *Rara avis*. My attempts to bend his illness, let alone to break it, involved me in as tough a challenge as I'd faced in my professional career. And whether bird or beast, or closer to the serpent, as he seemed, he teased me through a labyrinth of curves and twists and switchback turns that giddied me.

Why *serpentine*? Because he loved to stretch his fangs their full extent, then sink them deeply into those he bit. Poor chap! He probably never realized it was himself he hurt as much as any foe.

Why *rare*? Because his mind so scorned the commonplace it even dreamt in symbols all its own. To comprehend their message would exact the fullest strengths I had. His fantasies were woven into patterns both so weird and wonderful they might have been transcribed and sold intact as high-grade science fiction.

Oh yes, he meant for me to feel his sting when he proclaimed his plans to "end it all." Nor could I talk him out of it. He was impregnable. He had defenses strong as concrete walls. It didn't matter that I'd "cracked his code" and told him so, or, far more tragically, that underneath his armored scales he wanted so to yield, to let me make him well.

Ye Gods what stubborn pride and arrogance! I don't recall that ever with more zeal (or less result) I struggled to allay the pains of anyone.

But I anticipate.

I recollect the way that guy would curl up on my couch for hours on end, day in and out, with not so much as an uttered word—for weeks if he chose. Or how suddenly (with me off guard), he would hurl a thunderbolt or toss a nugget out, but quick and unobtrusively. I'd grasp it, if at all, in retrospect, and fruitlessly attempt to waylay him with insight on a trail by then grown cold.

Our first meeting is still as fresh in my mind as if it happened yesterday. He spoke his name, I mine. We shook hands, then sat. He smoked.

The bluish clouds came wafting out from somewhere deep within his chest. He didn't blink or even look about my room. His gaze instead found focus back behind my eyes—that feature too suggested he was cool, reptilian. His forehead frowned as if in grief, although as we talked, his body stayed postured as if cased in paraffin, allowing not a movement to be made to the slightest excess. Nor did he waste a word.

"How can I help?" I asked.

"It's changing that I need; I'm suffering. I'm miserable like this."

There was a clue. A gemstone. Five hundred analytic hours would polish and refine it. And juxtaposed, another diamond in the rough—his having backed his car, rear end first, up to our consultation. Bizarre approach.

Was I naïve to accept his glib answer that it gave him faster getaways once we were through, and that he thereby saved some precious seconds in his rush to, work? Or could that be a lightly-veiled charade bespeaking something far more sinister, unplumbed, and idiosyncratic? How could one know at first?

Then there was how he'd earned his living all those months by spotting tailgate drivers. Know what he'd do? He'd jockey into place around in front of them, and slamming on his brakes, he'd get himself rear-ended. Purposely.

Does that sound strange?

Limping from his car, he'd rasp a warning out about his hurting back. Then he'd suggest he didn't feel too good. "We'd better settle this ourselves without reporting it or else they'll hike your premium. Plus my way I don't have to sue you, chum, account of 'whiplash,' see?"

Once his victim left, he'd spring back in his car and race it home where he would weld the broken parts or change the bumper guard with salvage from the dump—gloating all the while upon his cleverness, and income taxes saved. Oh quite an *avis rara*, Karel!

In retrospect I can forgive myself for having misunderstood that "change me" had indeed implied considerably more than helping him in school or "making it" with friends and living normally. I'd probably again believe that simple avarice had spawned that freeway ruse and that his backing into port was only, as he'd said, just for efficiency. But, as I later learned, my patient was complex. His plea that he "be changed" contained a cryptogram. I'd break it down at last and tell him what he'd meant. How both those actings out were rooted in his youth; how both derived from years before acquired speech.

* * *

Karel was an only child. His earliest memories were of Providence, a gray, sooty, depressing East Coast city where his mother died when he was very small, and of his father's bitterness at needing extra work to pay her doctor bills. With his mother's demise, Karel was sent off to where luck found an empty crib, to the home of Uncle Toby who had lost *his* infant son.

Bleak choice. Still mired in grief, his sallow uncle could express scant love or tenderness for Karel's puissant needs, nor was any issued from an aunt or other relative. From none at all. Indeed, as I knit a fabric from the skeins of yarn he brought, the picture that emerged disclosed a little lad who lay for hours alone, neglected and ignored. Vast, boundless spaces stretched without a living creature's passing by to speak to, pat, or gentle him, to play a silly game or rock or coo or bounce the tiny guy. Supine or prone, his "diapers soaked in piss," he was obliged to wait until his father, tired and glum, dyspeptic at his best, might happen by to *change them.*

In consequence, these circumstances etched themselves as intrapsychic grooves in Karel's nascent mind, as imprints seeking *change.* This was the message he would voice once he had learned to speak, that he'd enact in soundless pantomime—presenting me *his rear* in backing to my door, or *changing* his own tail when someone banged it up. In fact, this would explain those silent, endless hours of lying on my couch, as if, regressed, he lived again the selfsame silent days in Toby's home, within that very crib.

There was the magic key to Karel's morbid code. But he'd expanded it to broader spheres, to where his trust faltered and left him loveless, suspicious of everyone.

At the depths of his analysis, I found my theory proved, but how it was received and what he chose to do unfold another tale—his final treatment hours.

*   *   *

Picture with me, as the curtain parts, a scene with Karel shuffling rubble on his desk. He'd built the desk from a door reduced in price because its surface had been scratched. Its black wrought-iron legs imparted an antique look. At first glance, the piece seemed somewhat elegant, but in fact was more "Jerry-built."

The room itself was as long and narrow as a dining car. Its shape obliged him to run the desk up tight against the wall. At the far end lay an army surplus cot and arctic sleeping bag—much to his Spartan bachelor style. At the other, squatted a plastic leather chair. Within its deep-walled lap he used to sit and read, play solitaire, or plan his schemes.

The whole tableau was cheerless, dank, and musty—a cell where he could sleep or rustle up the sustenance to keep his flesh alive and do his "handiwork." Yet, small and confining as it was, its clutter was overwhelming. Piles of junk stretched everywhere—like an archaeologic recording of all that he'd been busy with for months and months and months.

Look. Lidell and Scott's *Greek Lexicon*, reposing on some yellow onionskins for interlinear translation; *Hertz on Radio* (unread) balancing on a Pisa Tower of college "cribs," beneath which, struggling out, an octopus machine of cords and wires and gear-wheels of some diabolical device. There, on the left, another "dig": the entrails of a clock. From these young Dr. Frankenstein would make a fan next spring. And a broken toaster holding down the graphs on which he'd plotted stock commodities. Further back, the microscope and cameras, and all those soldered gimcracks, nuts and bolts of "Project Chess Set." Disorganized, Machiavellian, littered all around.

Have I to stress that Karel was unwed? Or that he lived alone? That no one ever visited him? His days were spent in school where, much like Tantalus, he kept reaching toward the coveted degree, without quite grasping it. At night, to meet his basic needs, he worked the graveyard shift in a local space industry.

Karel hated his job and the crew with whom he was obliged to pass those hours. Indeed, several times his acid manner and disdain had nearly cost him his job. Unknown except to a handful of associates, the man moved silently through space, unnoticed, and decidedly unloved.

I learned how come. To Karel live people were like billiard balls. He moved the ones he could, and when his duty or some fate necessitated it, not otherwise, he used to run along, beside, and bumping here and there make contacts, gingerly, at points. He never would allow himself to fuse or let his stuff amalgamate with theirs.

"I don't blend in; I can't trust 'letting go.' I'm water mixed in oil. You gotta keep me stirred. That way I look transformed, but later, when you stop, I split, intact, just like I always was."

Eddy was an example. He and Karel sat next to each other in second-half Psychology besides working at the same plant on the same shift. During lulls in the tiresome routines, Eddy, gregarious by nature, would attempt various conversational gambits.

Few succeeded, but on a particular evening, having been lectured to that very morning on nonverbal communications and ESP, Eddy, "turned on" by his subject, tried to engage Karel in a bull session. J. B. Rhine's research at Duke and Edgar Cayce, the so-called "prophet," had been cited. Eddy had been all ears. He reiterated to Karel bits of this and that as detailed in the lecture.

Karel snapped at him, "Christ Eddy, I was there."

"I know," said Eddy, "but did you really catch his act? Jesus, Cayce musta' been some devil!"

"Can it Eddy; turn it off!"

"I will," his sidekick offered, "but gawd I wish that I could see him once and pick his brain. Oh wow, I wish that he was still alive."

"He was pure fake," Karel echoed back for Eddy's efforts. "Just another con man, like the rest."

"Christ, you couldna listened, Karel! He predicted earthquakes and he cured arthritis. He could contact corpses."

"You're congenital or Mongoloid, you moron, Eddy. Take my word: those clowns are stuffed with shit. Only idiots and hysteric females get suckered by their line. Don't you know how they work?"

"Not Cayce, Karel. He was real."

"Real, my duff, you nincompoop. Science, now that's *real*, and nothin' else. Cayce, Cayce, Cayce. Next month I suppose you'll go to Lourdes. Hey, how's about I read those lumps there on your skull? Or all those v.d. sores on both your palms? Ah, what's the use? Why should I waste my breath?"

"Karel, you gotta admit that some things that he did were pretty hairy. You disagree?"

"I do, you simple jackass! All them monkeys work the same routine, with variations. They trick you into spilling info while you're off your guard, then they mix it in with generalities, a little luck, a little experience or intuition, and the Barnum thing in people makes 'em hear what they wanna hear. It's just shit!

"Look, you take Cayce's best feat and I'll give you some plausible ... in just one week ... say, I'll make you a bet. Oh, wait a minute chump. Whoa there! Wait a minute. You know what? In your super ignorance you just helped me stumble on one hell of an idea.

"Yeah. Eddy, you go back to Sapville. I have found myself a project ... not a bad one ... not at all."

Within minutes, Karel was threading his Triumph through the city streets toward his long and slender room. He was busy now with a cascade of creative thoughts interspersed with calumny, sometimes voiced aloud, for Eddy's naïveté.

Of course Karel had read about phrenologists and seers. Séances and ouija. But all wizards did their best work in some place to Hell-and-gone. With no one there to check them, or to validate results. Hmph! How reliable can data be if they are gathered up like that?

Well, the wheel turns. Karel's project was a beaut. Maybe he'd do a paper on it, or his Ph.D. Thinking which, he pulled up to his driveway, stopped, spun about, and backed into place.

However, heavy with fatigue, he decided to let all lie until morning. Kicking off his loafers, he unzipped his sleeping bag, postured just an instant at its side, then, fully clothed, released whatever held him and just melted within its plaits.

Undoubtedly Karel's psyche set to work as his earthly body rested. Somewhere deep within its convolutions was spawned the rough mold of "Project Debunk Phony." Its aims: to prove his scientific thesis, to advance him academically, to put Eddy down once and for all, and something else, for sure.

First he'd locate a self-professed fortune teller, then catch him in a lie, and impale him on it. But, he'd need strict purity of method, the rigors of a controlled experiment. Slowly; go slowly. Step by step. Yeah. See if the "hoodoo" could give him even one eensy-weensy fact for which Karel hadn't supplied the clues.

*   *   *

An old analytic dictum urges therapists to wait a respectable time before assessing the results of their treatments. Distance lends perspective. Karel's highly individualistic qualities always had me just a little disoriented and a bit off in my timing. At any particular moment I found it difficult to appreciate exactly what he was up to and why.

But when I heard the preamble to "Project Debunk Phony," I was virtually certain that it's other subtle, nefarious purpose related to the therapy and me. He'd never settle his accounts with just one bird for any single stone; not if he could clobber two or three or more. My hunch, albeit hazy, kept portending that not only the prophets and poor Eddy, but the "romantic sap" of the doctor as well were to get caught in his snares.

One other consideration is of note: after months of work Karel and I had hit a dry spell. His project followed upon a very lengthy, strained period of intensely stubborn silence. I had tried and tried to break it without success. Day after day he backed up to my office, lay down, and waited soundlessly until I'd end our "talk," some fifty minutes later. The quiet had become so palpable that if ever the telephone broke in, I would excuse myself, respond briefly, and then, returning to him, accurately, if paradoxically, I'd reply: "Yes, please, now continue"— which he did, without a sound.

Nothing in my armamentarium enjoyed the slightest success in penetrating his resistance. Then, for no apparent reason, Karel resumed speaking, but of his own resolve. His tone and manner suddenly mirror-imaged the arid stretch behind. He rained and poured the project out, nor would its flow be curbed.

It was meant to be an epilogue, it seemed, to struggling with his "case." Its message would be passed before me for inspection and then dropped, ticking like a time bomb at my feet. Perhaps my art would be ample to defuse it. I should see. If not, I felt for certain he was gone, beyond recall.

Just one word more: his rectitude. He was a kind of monster, yes, as if himself composed of all those springs and wires and pulleys from his "lab," but, and I counted heavily on this, I knew that I could depend entirely upon his love for honesty. He would present the facts in any story impeccably. Bitter, strange, sardonic, weird, they all described him, but I was utterly confident that he would relate to me the project in its true form.

*   *   *

Sunday.

All quiet.

Karel, fully clothed, fused within the folds of his sleeping bag, was snoring softly. Then, as if upon a stage, a subdued light gradually intensified.

Action.

In the midst of his junk pile a little gizmo began a rhythmic flip and flop. Back and forth. Perking motions, building, building, building, till at last the monster stirred. Roused himself and sat.

Karel blinked. He yawned, scratched at his body through his outer clothing, looked out, bit into an orange he'd left lying on the sill, and then, but half awake, began shuffling through the flotsam adrift everywhere on his desk—the very scene on which we focused pages back.

He was undeflected from his purpose of the prior evening. Aha! The phone directory! There he found "clairvoyants" midway past the letter "C." The only one, however, (curse the luck!) was a female tea-leaf reader who saw clients by appointment. Madame Sonya.

He wrote her number in a tiny spiral notebook, sat back, and lit a menthol to think.

The mainspring of his strategy must be to present this Sonya absolutely no fortuitous clue of his identity, past, interests, or ambitions. If she could fathom anything, *anything* at all factual, discounting luck or chance, it *might be divination*. If she could duplicate or triplicate that act, the likelihood of black art of some kind would increase exponentially. So, uppermost must be control of "leaks" from his person. A minimum of speech, lest accents reveal birthplace or training, and a paucity of motions. His appearance must be a paragon of blandness, the accomplishment of which meant scrutiny of the minutest details of his style and items of his dress, as well as all the rest.

Quick assessment of the limits of his wardrobe narrowed it to casual attire. Oxford-gray flannels might hint Ivy League. They'd intimate his student status. Better chinos. Similarly his corduroy jacket and brown velour pullover would be choice. No sense in wearing the sweater with the leather elbow patches; it was professorial.

Shoes? The loafers; certainly not sandals. And did socks matter? Well, pick a pair conservative in color. More important, carry neither magazines nor tell-tale pens or pencils nor match books that might hint at where he ate, shopped, or idled. And, damn it, smoking too was out. There was a stab! Karel knew his best performance in such crises usually hinged upon the tranquilizing suck of cigarettes. But what one smoked and how were giveaways to even semi-pros.

"Keep my hands as much concealed as possible," he reasoned. "She'll spot my grimy claws and sniff my hobbies out and student callus. Plus I don't wear rings" (not to mention that his nails were bitten to the quick).

That much for a start. The rest he'd ruminate on throughout the week of deadly routines down at the job—rehearse and re-examine, giving thought to closed-circuit T.V. and one-way screens, to peepholes and the like, with zest and rich imagination. In and out and up and down and once around again until his inner scientific monster felt it had, as near as possible, a rigorous design despite involving humans (not machines or rats). One week thence, on Saturday, he'd call, first thing.

The hours sped past. When D-Day dawned, our hero cleared a working space amidst the clutter, then dug out his spiral pad. He lit up and, dragging deep, etched furrows on his brow; pinkie skyward, he punched Madame's code. Pleasant tinkly tones responded to his touch. His pulses trotted unexpectedly; her number rang and rang without response. The monster moaned.

"Oh crap—she isn't in."

Just as: "Hello, here's Sonya. Who is dat?"

"This is, er, Mr. X," he cried. "I'm phoning for a reading. Can you hear?"

"Yeh, vot's your name? I hear."

Alert, he snapped, "No names just X."

"I'm all day, Mr. Eggs, come then."

With that the line went dead.

Unnerving to be cut off abruptly; it was unexpected, and irregular, not playing by the rules. That lousy "human factor" in experiment designs. But beyond a briskness of his manner, he had tossed out not one clue—so, move along.

It was a lovely, bright clear day: blue and cool and sparkly. All around was evidence of spring awakening, antithetic to the aged city's ugly winter. The air breathed hope and birth, perfume and promise. The weather sung of Haiku, music, romance, dreams. How little of that touched our hero. He sniffed the winds to guess the temperature, then smugly clucked to find that he'd been accurate. The beacon on Prudential's tower confirmed his nose thermometer within just two degrees.

From the address shown, 120 Weycross, Karel surmised that Sonya's office, or whatever, was in the older quarter; it could be a slum or a penthouse; no way to tell until there. He geared his pace to churn out just four miles an hour, then set his watch again to calibrate his speed. He slowed a little, though, as he neared a shop displaying leather goods.

He knew that place from having seen it several times before. Its windows always lured him in some strange, enchanting way. The "gestalt" he found appealing, not the items taken singly: cowhide flasks to secrete liquor, riding crops, toilet bags, and several styles of notebooks, trimly bound and monogrammed. Conventional, and nothing much in truth.

Next door, a French café, La Fleur-de-Lys, was tucked into the basement of an ancient former church. Made all of stone, the structure should endure millennia to come. In its window the menu, "bouillabaisse and escargots" (what were they anyhow?), set Karel to reflecting that he was almost uninitiated in French cuisine. In a blink he fell to pondering on Frenchmen and how much he loathed them.

Sissy waiters. Christ, they peeved him! One propitious day they'd be a "project" too, when he had time . . . but now . . . he'd better move.

The scheme he'd reckoned to outsmart a T.V. sensor called for walking briskly on the far side of the street. Once at Madame Sonya's level, a left-flank maneuver, and a dart right through her door should elude most spying lenses; but somehow in this much torn and rebuilt section all the numbers were awry. There were huge gaps in their series; then they came in clumps. Upsetting his plans further, suddenly he saw himself abreast 120, much too soon. Another gaffe. The rotten luck!

The building was a shambles, rundown, antiqued through neglect. In the foyer, tarnished brass mailboxes lined the wall; each had a buzzer and smudged nametag. Last of the lot, the pathetic logo advertising in longhand, "Madame Sonya—Two flights up. Wait." Ah, so, it seemed she had the top floor suite.

The passageway and climb were very long and narrow. The air was close and musty, strangely damp. Illegally steep risers made ascending quite a chore, somehow endless and unpleasant. Dimly lighted and unclean, the walls and ceiling blended where they came together, like a funnel to her door.

Could Karel be in such poor condition that despite his youth the exertion of that stairway made some fluid back up in his lungs? Or, could it be a heavy-hearted venture (not his smoking) that produced his little cough?

And then he tumbled on her waiting room itself. Out of the tunnel and into a box. He assessed its contents with his initial glance. It had a dingy, fraying wicker chair and a brace of dog-eared calling cards, as aged as the one below. No magazines or see-through mirrors; it was like a closet with a seat, excepting for the fly-specked floor-to-ceiling window that looked back down on Weycross and beyond.

"God, what a dump," he mused. "I guess I cloak-and-daggered things beyond all reason." Yet there was a puzzling smell; it could be incense; should he peek? Just then, at the far end of the cell, a beaded curtain jiggled, tinkled, and a heavy bumping noise behind it grew and grew until—with a swish the beads parted and there the *Madame Sonya* stood before his view.

What a most unlikely gypsy. What a plain straight-forward dame. She had the romance of an aging Jewish grandma—nothing more. Was this to be the sorceress he'd joust with? Shit! She was fat, not slinky. Instead of a flesh-tight shift with plunging cleavage, Sonya wore a baggy, torn, and faded smock. It wasn't from the Orient, just some bargain basement down the street. No ruby in her nose, no pins, no baubles; in fact, she had no jewelry at all except a wedding band, and something looking vaguely like a necklace around her throat. That, upon inspection, proved to be a slightly raised and rounded scar, wrinkled some with age.

One could only conjecture why Karel was so quick to spot it. But he did. It was the telltale vestige of an operation for a hyperactive gland, identical exactly to the one *his* mother'd had. He remembered how she'd suffered. He knew every pang by heart. Yeah, here was another unexpected.

Hers had been a keloid Karel touched and stroked and rolled beneath his fingers in his early memories (how few of them so clear). What trick of chance? What could this mean? Had Sonya suffered too? This harridan who said she could read tea leaves? Surviving, reaching such an age while young ones died?

*   *   *

"You are Mr. Eggs?" she asked, half knowing, and half telling him to follow where she led.

Through the beaded curtains they passed into a larger furnished room. Its unicellular arrangement provided for her eating, sleeping, living, and working. Its clutter paralleled Karel's own. She bade him sit, as slowly, still in silence, from around behind, she produced a steaming pot of tea. Another, gently simmering, in erratic cadence puffed out cabbage clouds from beneath its lid.

With surprising grace, Sonya procured two heavy porcelain mugs from an overhead shelf. Then somehow with a single movement, magically, she put silver on the table, and a napkin. Whereupon she poured, neatly filling his cup first, then hers.

"So, drink now, Sonny," she instructed, "Lemon, sugar later if you want. Empty. Not to stir the leafs. Then Sonya tells you what she sees."

" 'Sonny,' " he thought. "Cool it. Keep your cool. Do what she asks."

Karel leaned over the steaming cup, sniffed its aroma, dilated his hairy black nostrils, and did as told, but . . . it *was tea*—plain tea. From some local market, not the East.

"Now," said the seer, "careful, careful, not to move the leafs; I read."

Sonya studied the dregs. There, within the cup, a mash of moist, dark, green, nondescript residuum sparkled the overhead bulb in myriad, steaming hot reflections. Taking the utensil from him with authority, she tilted the rim to peer into its depths. Her facial furrows molded themselves into a giant brown and yellow prune. Her shiny, tight-skinned finger with its knobby knuckle traced first in and then around the edges soundlessly. For at least half a minute Sonya stared down into the deep, and for at least an equal time she then gazed at him. Uncomfortable and queasy, he too made no sound.

"You like tea, Mister?"

Somewhat off his guard he managed, "I ... er ... do I?"

"Look," she cried undaunted. "See, here, the letter 'T.'"

Karel peeked. It was a "T," no question, one leaf across its counterpart, perfectly perpendicular, a "T." "So?" he challenged.

"'T,' 'T,'" she continued. "It is maybe an important letter to you?"

Karel thought of Toby, his uncle-father-mother, his infancy factotum, and how in that very Toby's bedroom he had lain long and empty hours. All those dark and soundless eons in his cousin Sammy's crib, while his father scratched a living. With his mother in her grave. Was "T" supposed to summon all that forth? He blanched.

"*Tell me*, Madame Sonya," he protested. "You tell me," he cried again.

She blinked. "Heh, look, see? Here is 'T.' It makes the cross, one leg. Ah, yeh, maybe an 'X.' No, I don't think. 'X' could also mean, but this is 'T.' Try hard to think. Someone maybe dat you know?"

Composed enough to handle his annoyance, Karel snorted that the most frequently used letters in the language are first "E," then "T," but spoke no more, just glowered.

"Naagh, you think; it comes; anyway, here is water. That is sure. You and *water* too. I couldn't say for why, but look, so much. Vot else?"

He glanced back at the mash. Of course there was water—she had brewed the tea in it.

"So, does it mean an ocean voyage or a shower bath?" he shouted, but a hint of vertigo was rising in his ear. Thoughts again of infancy, of Toby, of how he hated to change diapers, and of how he himself had floated through those years in "piss and bilge" and—what was this? The room was growing warmer, little beads of sweat were filtering through his cologne. Two coalesced and dropped upon the table.

Sonya saw and winking, "You don't feel good maybe?" she essayed.

"Madame, Madame Sonya."

"Yeah?" she sighed.

"You have told me absolutely *nothing*—only questions."

"Yuh, you too, Sonny. Why you wouldn't say. You ask."

"What. Wait a minute, lady, you're supposed to give me answers. Jesus Christ, have you the gall?" he started, then choked up.

"Please?" she queried patiently and sat with her rheumy eyes upon him. She would have waited there forever had he not loosed his collar and cried out, "Now listen to me, Sonya; I came to see if you could tell *me* something, anything about myself, not *give* you all the facts. So far you've told me nothing; all *you've* done is pump me. You have got it backwards woman. So then, how's about it—if you can!"

"Something wrong, Sonny?" she asked him softly, sad-eyed, like a wounded doe.

"No, not 'Sonny,' dammit. I'm a *man*. A *scientist*. Ach, you got that from me. Listen you. I came here to experiment, to see if you could give me just one lousy little fact about myself, and all I've seen is tea-leaf Rorschachs. Madame, you are a quack. This thing's a bust."

Bleakly, eyes upon his temple, she observed a vein there swell and start to pulse. Karel felt it too. Waves of nausea telegraphed a migraine coming, which (when black spots danced before his eyes) brought on a little thaw in his intensity. Smiling thinly, and with effort, Karel tightly said, "Madame, continuing our—'reading'—scientifically will be a waste of time, for both of us."

To which, once again but ever gently, Sonya murmured, "Mr. Eggs, you ain't a friendly type; I wouldn't read you more. Naagh, better I don't tell your fortunes." And rising, she pushed her chair back toward the stove.

From the same shelf whence the cups and saucers, she produced a sugar bowl and started toward the fridge.

"You like some tea, but now with milk or lemon, just to drink?" she asked, as if the scene up to that point might simply fade out.

"So light as that?" Karel roared. "Sweet Jesus! Don't you understand me woman? You haven't told me anything so far. No, not a goddam thing! Can you guess my name? Or birthday? Where I'm from? Can you even figure what's my work?" He thrust his hands right up beneath her nose.

"You are a student, sure." she chuckled, her eyes glittering. "Chah, chah, chah! And also smart, but it's enough; Sonya doesn't more." With which she eased her hulk into the seat again, and seemingly resigned to search her tea for solace, muttered, "I wouldn't charge you . . . on the house."

"Charge me!" Karel wailed (the migraine twisting), "Ha. Charge me. Boy, you've got your nerve. Hey!

Wait a minute lady. Hey! I've got it. Don't charge me,
and I won't you. No, not a penny and *I'll tell you your
future*; it won't cost a cent."

"Tell me my?" she uttered, her face clouding, "Oi!"
Then sighing into space and trailing off, "Sonya ain't
got."

"Okay, sweetheart. Like you said it. So instead,
suppose I read you from your past?"

"Past what? Oi again! Today enough. Better
somewhere else," she said.

"Oh no. I'm going to put it all together for you,
Sonya. Instant past. But done with science, not your
damned hot water and your tea leaves. Karel will tell
all. See here."

But just then a funny recollection seized him. It was
of this mother, as he'd known her last. And, only a
slender membrane separated him from knowing that she
and Sonya would be the same age, if she had lived.
Magnetized, staring at the scar, and growing slightly
giddy, he sensed that cabbage mist began to fog the
air. Sonya shrank and somehow wizened. He could see
her in a coffin and with tortured looks. Then his
mother's life began in bits and pieces to float before his
eyes.

"Yes, I see it. Those days you were so slender and
they worried for your health, and how your voice got
hoarse, then how your hair fell out in fistfulls, and your
palms would drip with sweat. I see it all . . ."

And Sonya sat transfixed as he went on. She did
indeed recall them, every one. Could he be Aaron, the
boy who used to live downstairs? Grown up? How else
to know those symptoms? Or *was* he *magic*, really?

"Are *you* Aaron, Mr. Eggs, who lived downstairs?"

"Just listen, 'Mother.' I'll go on . . . You'd wake up in the morning and wonder what was changing in your face. How come that stubborn coughing when you climbed to your room? Ah yes, Sonya, Karel knows."

"True, all true," she muttered, "Every word. You have the gift!"

"Gift?" asked Karel with some smugness. "Not at all. Just an exercise in logical deduction, which wouldn't interest you. Applied science, Mother. Science, and some observation that you had your thyroid cut up years ago. I've just recited you your symptoms. Both before and after. Pretty neat."

Gloating, he busied himself with entries in the little ledger. Sonya, open-mouthed, could sense his gross contempt. She weakly asked him, "Who could tell you yours, so full of anger? Fortunes is for people with poems in their heads, not science."

"Ah, yes," said Karel, "and no doubt Eddy will have some similar excuse, but I do thank you for what turned out after all, a most diverting hour." And reaching into his pocket for a bill, "I guess I have to give you *something* for your trouble. Here, can you make me change?"

Sonya heard that. "Make him *change*?" How did he mean that? To *change* him, or to change *him*, or just to make change for him? She saw, with the wisdom of the aged, how babyish this Caesar was, this Caligula, as he stood there, and she wanted so much to tell him that "changed" indeed would suit his baby needs. Yet she could only stammer, enigmatically, that that was the problem with all of it, she couldn't, alas, make for him the kind of change he needed.

Again, it is very conjectural as to what Karel really

understood of that redundancy, and what Sonya did. He momentarily rethought of Toby, "T," water, urine, diapers, as he descended the steep stairway, but at the bottom, in the fresh spring air, nose high, he headed toward the leather shop, deciding with the dollar saved to visit La Fleur-de-Lys—to try those escargots and "case the waiters" for a "project." To seek new worlds to conquer and to flush this Sonya out. To restore it back to where it was before.

*   *   *

And, having heard it all, myself a bit transfixed, I wanted too a little to restore. From where I sat, looking down upon his ebon, curly locks and beyond to those flaring nostrils, at the body much foreshortened on my couch—tapered monster—I sensed what was to come. I was aware both what the tale had meant and why he chose to tell it. How right I'd been in anticipating bombs. And was I wrong, or had he told it as it really happened, even if to do so showed his quandary and the seer's quasi-skill? Bitter, brilliant boy.

At length I said to him, "Okay. You want to analyze that story or am I to make some comments on your plot?"

Not a whit surprised there came but silence in response. And knowing for sure from precedents that nothing else would come, and by this time quite cognizant that naught within my bag of tricks could shake it, I said our years of work together left no doubt his anecdote was meant to bait me, and impugn *my* art, to show he hated and mistrusted me with all the rest, that he implied by his analogy how twins, this Sonya and myself, confirmed his lack of faith in seers and analysts alike. It was my "magic" he'd impale and my prognostications that he ridiculed this way. "Resistance" to be sure—original but tough. I couldn't see a way.

My confrontations bounced right off his armor, not a dent, despite a dozen tries. "And I do believe your lying here like this reconstitutes your past in Sammy's crib, when truly you weren't able to form words or signal out to those who might have heard you. And I do believe you've transferred onto me the same mistrust that may have been appropriate back then, but neither Sonya nor myself deserves the calumny you bring down on our heads. It's senseless that you hate the world and all the people in it just because you were deprived when you were young."

To which in ultimo Karel did speak, but only to proclaim that he and therapy had "had it," and that while acknowledging my skill he had "to terminate" the "work" and so his life. Nor did appeal to reason or emotion sway him. He was gone.

Months later, through a roundabout, I heard that he had killed himself. Barbiturates, procured without prescription, hoarded surreptitiously, consumed as he watched his television (without sound, just pictures), lying silently upon his cot, alone. *Incontinent*, he soiled himself in death. And no one in the living world knew why save me.

He left a note. Its message had a little touch of kindness, of a sort, a way of hinting I'd been right (and maybe Sonya too) in most of what I'd plumbed, but pain was pain. Analysis would need too long, hence hurt too much.

The Karel-Monster died. He went to join his mother in her grave. For certain, there, eventually, inexorable time would wreak on him more changes than had life. And doubtlessly he'd fuse his parts, at last. Rest assured.

9
The Anatomy of a Moron

An old medical dictum urges that physicians avoid harming those they cannot help: *primum non nocere*. I have always lived by it, but several years ago in a courtroom I was obliged to testify that a young man whom I had examined was a *moron*. Dull, but not so dull as to escape the sting of that obnoxious term, he winced visibly as I pronounced it. The experience made me try extra hard to be conservative with diagnostic labels, even to euphemize a bit where doing so made sense.

Years later I was to have a second chance. Fate brought another boy to my attention on whom that same hated tag was going to be hung. His story follows.

Winner of the Jacques Brien Memorial Award Competition.

It shows how much my keeping that resolution was able to affect his life.

* * *

"F-UU, F-UU, F-UU."

Aggie gritted her teeth; four fingernails dug into her fleshy palm. Her husband would be livid. The leaflet from which she read trembled with her rage.

All "fails" and "double unsatisfactories." Mike, their son, in fifth grade for the second time, twelve years of age, was flunking every subject. When Barnes saw that report card he would sing his old refrain for sure: adopting "the moron" had been a colossal mistake. He'd warned her; *she* wouldn't listen.

Well, moron or not, Barnes was nobody to go around calling names, not while he was practically living off a Navy pension for a "nerve disorder" himself. *"Nerve disorder."* Humph! Aggie didn't care by what fancy title they called it. She knew a drunkard when she saw one . . . all too well.

God, oh God, what could she do?

Aggie should have left Barnes years ago. His drinking was impossible, and worse, that foolish phrase he'd read somewhere and quoted to justify it, that alcohol and he were "where the ordinates of fate had crossed his destiny's abscissa." Oh, those words! She hated them. She hated Barnes. She hated his myopic notion that adopting kids was what men did because of impotence, which more than likely was the reason Barnes had had to prove himself by spawning Bobby after they got Mike. But bring *that* subject up and he grew violent, just as she feared he would on seeing Mike's report.

So when he stumbled through the door, Aggie, seizing the initiative, barked, "Well, you made it home again, huh Ralph. What happened? All the bars close down? Don't pass out yet, Your Majesty. We're going to talk. Tonight. Hear? *Look!* Myron, *your* son brought these home. An F-UU for every class; it's his worst card yet. I knew that I could count on *you* for absolutely zero, so I made *my* decision; like or lump it, Mister, I'm taking Myron in the morning."

Barnes pried his eyes apart. Reflecting defeat more than fury they made a rather futile plea that he be spared the scene he knew would come.

His wife pressed on, "to the school clinic, and over your dead and drunken body if I must."

"Sweet Jesus, Aggie! That clinic's for the birds," he managed to protest. "Head shrinks! Pfui! They're a bunch of phonies—I should know; I saw one in the Navy. The big imbecile needs their service like a hole in his coconut. Christ Almighty!" Saying which, he fell back on the sofa, quite done in.

"Ralph, sighed Aggie, "You bum! The boy could use a *father* for a while, not a sponge like you. You goddam fool!"

And wound that far into her accustomed litany, Aggie spun the record round through the rest of its well-worn grooves, omitting not an expletive of its tirade. When done, she turned away on cue, ran sobbing to her room, announcing that she'd sleep alone in it, as Barnes, befuddled in her wake, just curled up on the spot. Meanwhile in a corner of the house, in the reverberating dark, a captive audience to all those

painfully familiar echoes, hero of its burden and main
character of our story, Myron.

                    *   *   *

   His appearance at our meeting the next morning
was pure Dickens. David Copperfield come to life.
He was dressed in a faded, dirty workshirt, lassoed
around the collar by a necktie long enough to be his
father's. Twisted backside to, it reached his knees.
Mike's bottom half was hidden in a pair of patchwork
jeans. Struggling to contain his growth and uniquely
layered with stains, they offered clues to where the boy
had been the last six months since laundering.
   Nature misdemeanored with his face: thick,
protruding lips encased a lifeless smile. His teeth were
spaced like pegs left standing in a cribbage board.
Sparse sideburns competed with blemishes in every stage
of evolution, and on top a tropical thatch roof resisted
all control. On either side, beneath it, two glowing, red,
everted ears stood out (like skewer knobs to roast his
porky flesh). A whole so unappealing that just to smile
and offer him my hand mustered all the discipline I had.
   Mike grunted when I asked, "How are you?" He let
me squeeze a limp left paw, as with his naked right he
wiped his nose.
   I fought antipathy and beckoned him to tag along
to see the toys we had and where I worked. Kids usually
were dazzled when they did. Why not? The clinic
playroom was stocked with puzzles, paints, crayons,
models, and games; it had stuffed and furry animals for
the youngest, lead soldiers for the brave, erector sets for
future engineers—in short, what any heart desired. But

alas, nothing that got a gleam from Myron. He just balanced on the threshold, dazed and undecided what to do.

"Come on in and have a look. Okay? Games help kids talk," I told him. "We can even make some up; you want to try? What say?"

"Uh, uh," he mumbled, " I mean, who wanted to come to this place anyway?" But as he spoke, he ambled up and did deploy a rifleman face down upon the ground, then stood there eyeing me.

"Well, didn't you?" I asked.

He grunted, "No," and glancing toward the door, "My mother made me."

"Huh! I didn't know that. If she did there's got to be some problem. This is a clinic. Know what that is?" I asked, positioning a few more soldiers into place around the one he'd left.

"Yeah, I watched 'em on T.V. I seen a story—dis kid, he was adopped, like me. I forget the rest. Hey, c'n I play wid dis gun?" Mike fired a salvo of ping-pong balls at my battle array, knocking the little men helterskelter.

Then, he continued, "Bobby ain't. He's a *real* brother. I mean, not adopped. I ain't got no *real* mother. I mean my *real* father, he was missin' inna desert, inna war," then abruptly, "Hey! I don't like ta talk. Look, I jus' got five F-UU's, so my mom brang me. You suppos'a get me better grades. So how long I gotta stay here anyway?"

I rocked my swivel chair and looked at him, puzzled, hoping he'd go on as most kids would. When he was silent several seconds I asked, "Better grades, eh? Any idea how?"

"No. I dunno," he frowned. "You suppos'a."

"True. But any help you give me would be great. It speeds things up. All right, let's see if I've got the story straight so far, okay? You got an F-UU in every class. That means you didn't know your subjects; you didn't work well or cooperate, and your mom, who's really your adoptive mom, brought you here so I could help you to do better all around. Is that what gives?"

"Yeah, I guess," he muttered, after which, with plenty of prodding, piece by piece, he unfolded to our mutual discomfort the awful tale of the awful night before. Its recitation left no doubt that I was dealing with an eleven-year-old youngster desperately in need of aid, but one whose low I.Q., suspicion, and poor motivation (along with little likelihood of any real support from his fragmenting family) made him as bleak a prospect as I'd seen.

I probably didn't hide the gist of those ideas in my lackluster invitation to a routine second meeting; nor in it, when it came around, were my first impressions changed at all.

Throughout that follow-up, whenever I suggested that we play, Mike shrugged me off. If I left him alone, he just gazed blankly at the wall. If I asked questions or told stories, he was listless, inattentive. He had nothing to discuss nor did he give a hint of a direction. Indeed, he made me feel that therapy, were it to "happen," would need be one that reached into his limbo and then dragged him out besides—which in effect was my synopsis to our clinical director. He privately agreed, but, much moved by Myron's mother, yielded to her pressured pleas, not mine. Her doggedness squeezed from him a promise that I'd "make a stab" to see what could be done.

*   *   *

Today, I'd probably object to such an assignment to a child. It's difficult enough to work in optimal conditions; but if something fails to click right at the start, the chances are it never will, however hard you try. The chemistry should be right at the very first meeting. When it isn't, there's an uphill battle all the way. True, in theory, positive or negative prejudices should be analyzed and dealt with, but in practice, first impressions mostly follow to the end. Together Mike and I had scored near zero. To lift things off the ground would be some chore, although my distaste for his challenge was tempered by the thought that no one else was apt to like him any better; he had no other place to go. Besides, his situation looked so hopeless, even a small success would be a feather in my cap.

So we started.

At four o'clock each Friday, after school, Mike was dropped outside the door. Smiling blandly I would fetch him, ever watchful to discern his state of mind. It didn't vary. He was vapid, passive, logy, following behind me like a lump. In the playroom he was lifeless, as uninspired as anyone I'd ever seen or met.

Our times together, at first just dull, quite soon grew frankly painful. I should have understood his resistance. I was trained. However, gradually my resentment of him was deepening and, with it, profound regrets over the commitment I had made.

His teachers had the same complaints. A tutor called Mike "hopeless." Make-up tests, extra assignments proved futile. Nothing helped. He dozed over homework as if anesthetized, seemed numb in classes.

And his sessions at the clinic were almost more than I could take, as a frightful result of which, like it or not, even I, his last resource, was being inched toward giving him his father's kiss of death and sealing his chart with a Greek or Latin diagnostic label that would translate into "hopeless moron."

Do doctors think of quitting? Yes. Who wouldn't? Weekly I soliloquized ways to declare our joint agony foolish, yet hating so to brand him, I forced myself to put it off at least until our summer break.

A lot can happen over holidays. His family, so fragile in its structure, might split or move away. The boy could die. Sometimes clinics aren't refunded; it might lock its doors that fall. Or maybe, as I knew I ought, I could resolve why "taking this kid clinically" was proving such an awesome job.

*   *   *

In the early days Freud had his clients tag along when he vacationed lest there be a break in treatment. Later that practice was reversed; in fact, I was taught that patients after hours are "put away" and "kept there" until the next face-to-face encounter.

For most of my following, out of sight *was* out of mind, but Myron, well, he obtruded into my walks along the beach, between the soapsuds of my showers, and was "heavy" in a half a dozen dreams. If I saw kids with runny noses or teeth missing or read a blurb on retardation, he'd flash by; the very silence of my summer idyll would recall those painful quiets of our playroom meetings, until it dawned on me that I'd been fighting off the essence of his challenge. I had missed the forest for the trees. Mike was using me the way he used all the others, testing me before he'd place his trust.

So, when autumn rolled around and through his mom's manipulation he was first in line (bigger, dirtier, fuzzier, and fatter than before), I wasn't really sorry. Even when he absently replied he had "done nothin" since I'd seen him, and that he'd little to report, I plied vacation's strengths to rise to greater heights.

His family was "fine." He'd got new teachers, but he couldn't recall their names, their subjects, or what they looked like, which sounded distressingly familiar. However, I didn't let that dissolve away the skeleton on which I'd planned to build. Anticipating Halloween, I thought that holiday might be exploited. What could we lose? I wondered if Mike would like to make a mask for trick or treat?

"It could be fun," I suggested gingerly. "What do you say? Is there some kind you would wear if you went on the streets?"

"A monster face, like this," Mike smiled, exciting me with his rejoinder and then again when he switched expressions, even though his look was pained.

"Wow! That's a scary face," I offered. "What do you think we'll need to work on that?"

"Ah, I dunno. Forget it; never mind, it's stupid," he trailed off, and sinking in his seat again went blank.

"Hey Mike, you sounded eager for a second. Come on, huh. You want some paper? Crayons? Here, I'll help you, or even watch me if I start. Okay?"

"We could draw it onna paper 'n' cut it out," he said, "but, I dunno. My mom prob'ly won't lemme. Las' year I hadda snuk out. Could I scare kids wid my monster mask?"

"You bet! Say Mike, I think we're finding something to your liking. Monsters, huh. A lot of kids. . . ."

"Yeah," he said, "Frankemstein, Dracala, all them. I seen movies. Wanna see another scary face?"

And after that (his record monologue to date), Mike screwed his mouth and eyes and nose into a smirk, and held it as I watched. Though I could only wonder at its meaning, I thrilled at his involvement in some game, at long, long last.

Grunting, groaning, with his tongue stuck out to help him cut, at length Mike held his prize aloft. Obviously pleased, he laughed. The crudeness of the crafting dampened neither his nor my enthusiasm.

"Well, that's really something," I equivocated.

"Yeah, an' I'm gonna take it home. I mean, I can, okay? My maw says I can go to *Dracala*. He's a monster. Watch. Here's how he looks."

Stretching up to more than his full stature, Mike clawed the air growling through a half-closed mouth. His grimace fused into the mask's as he ran and stumbled toward the toy soldiers standing on the floor.

"Dracala, Dracala," he shouted. "All de mens get kilt. On'y this guy, they thought he was dead, see? But he wasn' [picking up one left lying], so he gets up an' shoots Frankemsteim—ack-ack-ack right inna eyes."

"Whoa! Back up a minute Mike. Dracula, Frankenstein? What story are you telling?"

Ignoring me, "Yeah! Ack-ack-ack! Frankemsteim an' everyone tho't he was kilt, see? Dead; he fooled 'em, 'cause really he wasn't. C'n I take de mask home?"

"Sure Mike, only I'm going to have some questions for you later about this Dracula-Frankenstein business.

It's all mixed up, like you put two stories together to make them into one of your own. Know what I mean?" Well, Mike was not about to enter such an academic orbit. Masks were on his mind and Halloween; best leave it there. I walked him to the door and said, "I'll see you," reflecting how exceptional it was that in our long acquaintance I was really looking forward to the next encounter.

In it I intended to re-examine the rare enthusiasm and the strange amalgam that had synthesized a soldier-hero who returned from death. Both might just explain some of the little guy's history and playroom behavior. With luck, they might be a Rosetta stone to his silent hieroglyphic. Some hazy good sense could be made of an adopted orphan's fabrication of a hero. He had use for one, God knows! It figured too, that he would identify himself with such a superman to borrow the strength and courage that he needed to slay the monsters of his private hell. Provocative, exciting, constructive thoughts. I wanted to test them out when next we met.

*   *   *

Mike had planned it otherwise. He may have sniffed my closing in and shied, or something else; I couldn't tell. He was the Mike of old, as tightly coiled up on himself as he had ever been, or maybe worse, despite the fact that just one week had elapsed.

Nothing, nothing, nothing I devised or conjured up could draw out a clue of what had happened in the interim, nor flash again the sparks we'd struck off with the mask. Even invitations to restore the battle scene met stony stubborn silence.

A week later, two, three, the impasse hung there. Lost in a funk, the boy was inaccessible, even somewhere back behind where we had started—mired down deep. I pitied those who suffered him for more than just one weekly meeting. He must have been intolerable, utterly.

Then an odd thing happened. During his next visit, Mrs. Barnes buttonholed me, impromptu, to report that Mike had acted "strange" some days before. He and his brother had been playing in the park. Mike banged away at Bobby from behind a boulder, then suddenly let loose the most unearthly scream she'd ever heard. He clutched his bosom, screwed his face up, and fell and lay there as if dead. Alarmed, she ran to help but Mike leapt to his feet with still another cry, "Ha! Fooled ya, didn't I? Ya tho't I was dead. Hurt 'n dead. Didn't ya?"

Could I tell her what went on? Was he worse?

I urged her to let me think it over, and talk with Mike before I made a guess. Later, in the playroom I silently sat a minute, hands folded, looking at my patient, considering the story I'd just heard. I repeated it verbatim, paused, and gave him option to explain—not a syllable or an eyeblink in response.

"Okay," I wound up, "then I'm going to give you my ideas. Listen hard because things really start to fit together and in a way that maybe ties it up for you, and your future, and school. Maybe even what you've been so damned hung up on that you can't even talk or play or anything at all. Just listen. Don't talk; try to understand.

"Remember what we discussed a while back, before

this park thing, you know, the Dracula story? With the soldier, the hero that they thought was dead?"

"Naw. I dunno nothin'; I don't wanna hear it either," he grunted. Then he grabbed the ping-pong gun and for several minutes ack-acked our entire perimeter. One of the balls ricocheted off his breast. He let out a loud long scream, clutched his chest, fell, and with a weird expression, lay there totally inert. Then he leapt to his feet and chuckling cried, "I fooled ya didn' I? Bet ya tho't that I was really dead."

He went through the same behavior, with little variations many times, refusing to let me continue along the lines of discussion I had opened. He didn't want to hear, I felt, and so I let him go.

For me, though, that charade clinched it. I understood all the data we'd collected and how they framed a plot that dovetailed his whole life into one piece. I could and would interpret his telling me that he was adopted, his play with guns and soldiers in our lab, his fictitious hero who returned from death to do in Dracula, the mask, the grimacing, the park, and finally this rerun for me, resurrecting someone who came back. Yes, two years of detective work to nail my villain, but I was sure I had him. I would strut the stage and sing my song the first chance I should get.

* * *

Guess what. At the time of our appointed meeting, I had to do my solo to an empty waiting room, that day and all of them thereafter; Mike would come no more.

Recalculating the family budget, Barnes, his father, had suddenly realized he was losing upwards of a fifth of Scotch each month by paying for treatment. Continuing was clearly foolish. "Head shrinkers," in his restricted view, were just plain "stupid." Having seen one in the Navy, he knew; whatever else might be said, the boy was still no better for the time and trouble and investment. Besides, what kind of therapy could take so long? Anyway there was no cure for *morons*. Didn't I know?

Well, I had planned to cope with Mike's resistance, but his father's was beyond my bag of tricks. So, close up shop. No argument would sway him, not even pleas for just one farewell session, "on the house," to make my summing up.

Console yourself, Doctor. No one wins 'em all. Don't let Barnes get to you. Within the hour, clinics being what they are, you'll find replacements rushing in to fill Mike's vacuum. Who knows? Maybe they'll be easier besides. That too is part of the objectivity one should have learned with one's diploma, eh? You're neither Jesus Christ, nor Sigmund Freud—and don't forget it!

I filed Mike's folder with a footnote, "Outcome indeterminate," and probably to retaliate, in part, wrote, "Case closed against advice," a bit consoled at having my personal aversion toward Mike turned around to something positive, akin to love of all his flaws and foibles. What a funny twist!

As the weeks passed, from time to time I'd resurrect Mike's ghost and recite to it the undelivered script. Occasionally I fantasied his dropping out of classes anyway, despite my message, a failure to the end. More often I'd construct a happy coda in which, somehow, he attended to the trials of school's career with the insights

I would have given, and without an albatross still hanging round his neck.

Kids with pimples or an F-UU, articles about resistance—almost anything could trigger the sad empty feelings of unfinished business, of a job undone. Then, in the midst of one such reverie, out of the blue, a frantic Aggie Barnes was on my line to speak of Mike's "arrest."

Between her breathless gasps were the terms of Mike's probation. His crime? According to the story, he'd seduced a little guy who lived just up the street. His sentence? Psychotherapy with me, if I'd accept him.

"Please bring him in," I ordered. And she did.

*   *   *

Well, my delight at still another chance was in no way mirrored in what sat before me once again. Nor was I really sure about the best way to begin.

I jockeyed, "Mike, your mother told me the whole business. Even so, I'd like to hear it from your lips. I think it's got an angle just the two of us would understand. So will you try?

"C'mon! I'm not the cops, or sheriff, or the judge; I guarantee that I won't scold you.

"Besides this is private, not the clinic. We've got to work fast. The very second the court lets him, your dad will stop us. It costs a lot to see me this way and he may not like that, huh. What do you say?"

Mike blinked, then struggled through a confession which smacked of "irresistible impulse." He let me tease out how, while playing soldiers with the youngster, he'd suddenly reached out and hugged and kissed and petted the little boy. Nightmarish regrets impelled his swearing him to secrecy, but that promise was not kept. No way!

Contrite and scarlet, Mike nodded, "Yes," there had been other times the same thing happened since our interruption; each was tied to loneliness and each involved his comforting some forlorn playmate, younger than himself. After which remarkable elaboration it was not the least surprising that he wanted a respite nor that I indulged him.

Handing crayons and paper to the wraith, I watched as he began a sketch—a tranquil scene, unpeopled, in the tropics, one which I thought might be medicinal, a counteraction to the chaos of his plight, a place where peace of mind prevailed. Had he been an "ordinary" patient I would have let him draw, then later analyzed his work. But when Mike drew still more palms and still more desert, sensing urgency, I played my hunch with everything I had.

"Mike, I'll bet that's Libya; it's where your real dad disappeared. Just look here at this picture. There's *absolutely no one there and that's the story of your life.*"

He snatched it, blurted in a breath that it was just a stupid scene, that I was stupid too, that he hated me, and always had, and that it wouldn't matter if Barnes should intervene and stop us. But he didn't slow me down at all. I had a toe pried in his doorway. I intended pushing through it then and there.

"Okay, if that's the way you want it, but first you'll hear what I've been waiting now for all these many months to say. Your story is so crystal clear that neither one of us can fail to understand it. You be quiet, then I'll let you talk; besides, I don't believe one second that you hate me any more than I hate you. Quite the reverse.

"You told me on the first day when we met that you had been adopted; you remember? And, you started shooting with that ping-pong gun to show me you could be a soldier too. And then that Dracula and Frankenstein affair you put together so that dead guys came to life, and the trouble in the park, and then the game of it you played with me back in the clinic, you recall?

"Mike, you're living out the story of your *father*. You want him to appear to take you out of here. That's why you hugged and 'loved up' little Timmy. *That's just the way you wish your father or his ghost would do to you.* Don't tell me you don't understand my message 'cause you do, and I'm going to repeat it to make sure. It's the most important lesson of your life. And I'm the only person in the world right now to teach it."

And I did, believe me. I interpreted the palms as a reminder that his biologic dad was listed as "missing in action" in Africa in World War II. To gild my lily, I extrapolated that he'd brought me back in a revival of the kind he'd wanted for his dad. I intimated that such wishes were so strong his mind had little energy for hobbies, school, or friends, or any damned other thing. Just coping day by day was draining him quite dry, which explained the F-UU's, the lack of friends and interests, the silence.

Ideas like that then tempted me to speculate aloud that he might be brighter than he'd realized, and get some better grades, be happier, show interest instead of drifting as he'd done in outer space.

Nor did I blurt it out a blink too soon.

"He's off probation, Doc," Barnes gloated, "I just fixed it. He won't have to go no more, so kiss him off."

Nor did I fight him (was there any use?). Or Mike's chart either, to which I tacked a "somewhat" where I'd written "against advice," a little more fulfilled in having got the message more across than I had done before. With further work I could have glued it fast. I might have shown him how the two of us, myself with him and he with me, had re-enacted the abandonment, mistrust, and resurrection story of a boy who loved and missed the image of his father, but, well, that was how it went. At least I'd jolted him a bit in his trajectory; he could come back to earth. The seeds of insight could now germinate in good conditions. I would never learn...

Or would I?

*   *   *

Again by phone, one more surprise, this time in tones deep and authoritative. Two years had passed— he'd be fourteen, at least.

"Remember me?" Mike asked. "I called to let you know *it worked*. I'm fine, and I wrote a poem on some stuff we talked about."

"A poem, Mike?" I gasped.

"It's going to be published in our paper here at school. I thought you'd like to see it. You want to, huh?"

"Of course," I choked. "There's nothing I would more. For sure."

And he sent a copy, late enough to make me wonder if I'd dreamt it. I gobbled up its message several times, with hunger and a thrill. It was a clumsy rambling effort that would never win him laureates. It rhymed but little, had scant meter, and yet was moving, utterly. Mike had woven into a recognizable fabric the insights I had scattered through his thoughts. Apparently I'd sprinkled them in soil more fertile than I'd ever fancied; they were taking root in very robust ways. No, I couldn't predict what ultimately was to burgeon, silk purse or sow's ear, that would have to wait upon more seasons, but one thing was sure, the "autopsies" performed on everyone, on Aggie, Barnes, his dad, the boy himself (and me), had freed Mike from the moron's role fate thrust upon him and had given him a chance to live *his* life.